D1625847

GRAND SLAM
CHAMPIONS

1908
1911 1909
1950 1952
1971
1978 1976
2008 2005
2012

FOREWORD

Grand Slam Wales in great shape for what lies ahead

The photographs in this book celebrate a significant milestone on an incredibly important journey for Welsh rugby.

Each page tells the story of how Wales won their third Grand Slam in eight years and sheds some light on what it takes to be the best.

Winning a Grand Slam writes a memorable chapter in sporting history, but there are other factors relevant to this squad.

What Wales achieved during the RBS 6 Nations Championship in 2012 was clear evidence that the systems and strategies in place are working.

This is a young squad recruited from talent developed along the WRU's elite player pathway which is now achieving meaningful success.

Young Welsh players new to senior rugby are emerging with the right skills and in the proper condition to contest at the highest level.

The personnel in place along that pathway and in the senior national squad, have undoubtedly proved their worth to Wales.

Securing Warren Gatland and his core team until beyond the next World Cup has shown to be fundamental to our long term development.

At the 2011 Rugby World Cup, this young squad proved that they have already developed many of the skills and confidence to challenge the best.

In the RBS 6 Nations, the players proved they can also achieve the ultimate sporting goal of any team and become winners.

That confidence and determination is based on a work ethic and determination we should all be proud of.

I know how hard the coaches and backroom staff work and I know how well the players respond to the challenges they are set on a daily basis.

Success can never be guaranteed in sport, but this team leaves nothing to chance in the level of preparation they go through before every game.

This book offers a unique insight into that preparation and gives a glimpse of the atmosphere created inside the camp.

We are all proud of them and grateful for what they have already achieved so far and genuinely wish them well for the exciting challenges ahead.

Roger Lewis
WRU Group Chief Executive

'In the RBS 6 Nations, the players proved they can also achieve the ultimate sporting goal of any team and become winners'

Hard work and commitment has made a nation proud

'I know what rugby means to the people of Wales and I know how much hard work and dedication these players have given to the cause'

I want my players to remember this Grand Slam as a vitally important milestone on an incredibly important journey for Welsh rugby.

They are predominantly a young team with a lot of challenges ahead and I know they can develop and grow from the achievements of the RBS 6 Nations Championship in 2012.

Most of these players are young enough to look ahead to the next Rugby World Cup and I know many of them are still smarting from what might have been in the last one.

They must take credit today for making a nation proud.

I know what rugby means to the people of Wales and I know how much hard work and dedication these players have given to the cause.

They are young men who have sacrificed a lot of the things other young people take for granted and they have never shirked on commitment.

Before a ball was kicked in this tournament we took them to a training camp in Poland at a training facility devoid of distractions and where the wintry conditions made for a gruelling environment.

These young men proved their calibre there and learnt from the experience.

In some of the games during this tournament we faced low points during which many teams might have given in.

These players showed true grit and fought back to victory in each and every game.

They did that in the face of great public expectation which would not tolerate defeat lightly.

I know the level of intensity we impose on the training camps and I know the pressure these players face up to day in and day out.

They have proved themselves to be both physically and mentally strong.

The manner of their victories has shown they have the skill to develop into an even stronger squad in the future.

While the majority of the current squad are very young, we could not have achieved this latest Grand Slam without the invaluable input from the more experienced members of the squad. They already knew what it took to achieve this kind of success and imparted that knowledge to the others off the field, and led by example on it.

I know there is still a lot of hard work ahead but I look forward to it with confidence and enthusiasm.

I want to thank our fantastic fans for their support and promise them we will all give every ounce of effort we can to make this Wales squad the very best it can be.

Thank you.

Warren Gatland
WRU Head Coach

INSIDE THE CAMP
WALES GRAND SLAM 2012

CONTENTS

INTRODUCTION

Blood, sweat and cheers – the story of our 6 Nations sensations...

The Welsh Grand Slam of 2012 was a story of perspiration as much as inspiration, as careful planning, hard work and sheer bloody-minded determination, allied to thrilling, emerging talent, brought deserved glory to Warren Gatland's men.

Although the clean sweep of the RBS 6 Nations Championship was the culmination of a superb 12 months for the national team, it feels like we are only just beginning to witness the potential within this magnificent group of players. The best may be yet to come.

We are fortunate to have an outstanding coaching and backroom team to support the men on the field. Years of preparation have led to the current success.

The World Cup in New Zealand last autumn brought Wales tantalisingly close to the ultimate prize, with only a heartbreaking single-point loss to France preventing us from facing the hosts in the final.

In teams of lesser character, the nature of the defeat could have led to a collapse in momentum and morale. Instead, it simply hardened the resolve to achieve greater things.

It is fair to say that the Grand Slam squads of 2005 and 2008 were surprise winners and had not been burdened with excessive expectation before those tournaments.

For the 2012 vintage, it was different. Performances at the World Cup raised the nation's spirits but also ensured Wales were installed as favourites before the RBS 6 Nations began. The pressure was on from the start and a fixture in Dublin was not a low-key way of opening the competition.

A thrilling encounter ensued. The lead changed hands five times as Ireland and Wales gave full expression to their attacking intent. George North was immense, scoring a try of his own and creating another for Jonathan Davies but we still found ourselves a point down entering the final minute. However, heads remained cool and a penalty was won that Leigh Halfpenny calmly slotted between the posts for a 23-21 victory.

Gwaed, chwys a chodi calon – hanes ein 6 Gwlad ryfeddol...

Roedd chwys ac ysbrydoliaeth yn gymaint rhan o Gamp Lawn Cymru 2012, wrth i gynllunio gofalus, gwaith caled a phenderfyniad dygn, ynghyd â thalentau gwefreiddiol newydd, ddod â llwyddiant haeddiannol i ddynion Warren Gatland.

Er bod llwyddiannau ysgubol Pencampwriaethau 6 Gwlad yr RBS yn uchafbwynt 12 mis aruthrol i'r tîm cenedlaethol, ymddengys ein bod dim ond yn dechrau gweld y posibiliadau sydd o fewn y grŵp cyffrous hwn o chwaraewyr. Gallai'r gorau fod eto i ddod.

Rydym yn ffodus i gael tîm neilltuol o hyfforddwyr ac arbenigwyr i gynnal y dynion ar y cae. Blynyddoedd o baratoi a arweiniodd at y llwyddiant presennol.

Daeth Cwpan y Byd yn Seland Newydd yr hydref diwethaf â Chymru o fewn trwch blewyn i'r wobr eithaf, gyda cholli o un pwynt yn erbyn Ffrainc yn ein rhwystro rhag wynebu'r tîm cartref yn y gêm derfynol.

Mewn timoedd llai o gymeriad, gallai natur y trechu fod wedi arwain at golli momentwm a chalon. Yn hytrach, fe gadarnhaodd y penderfyniad i gyflawni campweithiau.

Teg dweud bod elfen o syndod wrth fuddugoliaethau carfanau Cymru yng Nghamp Lawn 2005 a 2008 ac na fu'n rhaid iddynt ysgwyddo disgwyliadau'r cyhoedd cyn y bencampwriaeth.

Roedd pethau'n wahanol yn 2012. Cododd perfformiadau Cwpan y Byd ysbryd y genedl a sicrhaodd hefyd mai Cymru fyddai'r ffefrynnau cyn i Bencampwriaeth 6 Gwlad yr RBS ddechrau. Roedd y pwysau ar Gymru o'r cychwyn ac nid gêm ddibwys i agor y gystadleuaeth oedd yr ornest yn Nulyn.

Datblygodd brwydr wefreiddiol. Newidiodd y tîm ar y blaen bum gwaith fel y mynegodd Iwerddon a Chymru eu bwriad i ymosod. Roedd George North yn aruthrol, yn sgorio cais ei hun a chreu un arall i Jonathan Davies ond cawsom ein hunain bwynt ar ei hôl hi ym munud derfynol y chwarae. Fodd bynnag, pwyll piau a rhoddwyd cic gosb i Gymru ac yn gwbl hamddenol ciciodd Leigh Halfpenny'r bêl rhwng y pyst i sicrhau buddugoliaeth 23-21.

Wedi curo'r Alban yng Nghaerdydd, dangoswyd unwaith eto'r gallu i bwyllo a chynhaliwyd y gred yng ngallu'r tîm yn Twickenham, achlysur arall pan oedd Cymru ar ei hôl hi a dod i'r brig yn hwyr yn y gêm. Roedd

INTRODUCTION

After Scotland were beaten in Cardiff, the ability to remain calm and maintain belief in the team's ability was demonstrated again at Twickenham, another occasion where Wales came from behind late in the game. A high-quality contest had entered the final 10 minutes when another Halfpenny penalty brought the scores level. Then Scott Williams ripped the ball from Courtney Lawes, kicked ahead and collected before joyously diving over the line for a match-winning try.

The Triple Crown had been secured and everything was set up for the final two fixtures, back home at the Millennium Stadium. Italy were beaten before France, who just about held Wales at bay in the World Cup semi-final, provided the opposition in the RBS 6 Nations finale.

It was a tense afternoon but the men in red deservedly prevailed. Alex Cuthbert was to the fore again, scoring the only try of the game to make it three in three home fixtures for the young winger.

Wales were never able to establish a clear margin but seven points was more than enough as Gatland's side controlled possession in the final stages. The final whistle prompted a shuddering roar within the stadium and across the country as we acclaimed an 11th Grand Slam in our proud history.

This book had unprecedented access to the Wales national team set-up immediately before and during the tournament. It documents the blood and sweat spilled to make the Grand Slam possible, and includes the story of the triumph told, in their own words, by the men who made history.

After a look back at the oh-so-close World Cup campaign, we join the boys at their training camp in Poland during the depths of winter and eavesdrop on their intense weight-training sessions, exhausting routines on an icy beach, as well as witnessing them swimming lengths of a pool and entering the freezing cryogenic therapy chamber.

From there, it is on to the RBS 6 Nations championship with stunning images from the team coach, on the training pitch and inside the dressing room before and after games.

We see the aches and pains, strains and stresses, not to mention the elation and exhaustion, following 80 minutes of intense, brutal and compelling combat on the rugby pitch as Wales vanquished all their opponents with ruthless professionalism.

There is a particular focus on the final game against France as we see the players swap the red shirts for tuxedos ahead of the official celebratory dinner.

Inside The Camp: Wales Grand Slam 2012 pays tribute to the dedication and desire of all involved in the achievements of our rugby heroes. May there be many more chapters written in the years to come.

gornest o safon uchel wedi cyrraedd y 10 munud olaf pan ddaeth cic gosb Halfpenny â'r pwyntiau'n gyfartal. Yna rhwygodd Scott Williams y bêl oddi wrth Courtney Lawes, ciciodd hi ymlaen a'i chasglu cyn plymio dros y llinell ar gyfer y cais a sicrhaodd yr oruchafiaeth.

Roedd y Goron Driphlyg yn ddiogel a'r llwyfan wedi'i osod ar gyfer y ddwy gêm derfynol, nôl gartref yn Stadiwm y Mileniwm. Curwyd y gwrthwynebwyr yng ngemau terfynol Pencampwriaeth 6 Gwlad yr RBS, Yr Eidal yn gyntaf, yna Ffrainc, a gadwodd Cymru rhag llwyddo yn rownd gynderfynol Cwpan y Byd.

Roedd yn brynhawn llawn tyndra ond yn haeddiannol fe orfu'r dynion yn y crysau coch. Daeth Alex Cuthbert i'r brig unwaith eto, gan sgorio unig gais y gêm, gan sicrhau tri chais mewn tair gêm gartref i'r asgellwr ifanc.

Methodd Cymru ag ehangu'r pwyntiau rhwng y ddau dîm ond roedd saith pwynt yn fwy na digon wrth i dîm Gatland reoli'r meddiant yn y cyfnod terfynol. Cododd bonllef fuddugoliaethus o'r stadiwm, a atseiniwyd drwy Gymru gyfan, i gri'r chwiban olaf fel yr hawliodd Cymru â balchder yr 11eg Camp Lawn yn ein hanes.

Roedd gan y llyfr hwn fynediad digyffelyb i holl weithgarwch tîm cenedlaethol Cymru cyn ac yn ystod y bencampwriaeth. Mae'n cofnodi'r chwys a'r gwaed a gollwyd cyn gwneud y Gamp Lawn yn bosibl, ac mae'n cynnwys hanes y fuddugoliaeth, wedi'i adrodd yng ngeiriau'r dynion a wnaeth hanes.

Wedi syllu nôl ar ymgyrch colli-o-drwch blewyn Cwpan y Byd, fe ymunwn â'r bechgyn yn eu gwersyll hyfforddi yng Ngwlad Pwyl yn nyfnder gaeaf a chlustfeinio ar eu sesiynau codi pwysau dwys, ymarferion llafurus ar draeth rhewllyd, ynghyd â'u gweld yn nofio hydoedd o bwll a mynd mewn i'r siambr therapi cryogenig fferllyd.

Oddi yno, ymlaen i Bencampwriaeth 6 Gwlad yr RBS gyda delweddau trawiadol o'r garfan ar y bws, ar y maes ymarfer ac o fewn yr ystafell wisgo cyn ac ar ôl gemau.

Gwelwn y poenau, y pwysau, heb sôn am y gorfoledd a'r lludded, yn dilyn 80 munud brwydr ddwys, fileinig a grymus ar y cae rygbi fel y gorchfygodd Cymru'i holl wrthwynebwyr gyda phroffesiynoldeb didostur.

Mae canolbwyntio arbennig ar y gêm derfynol yn erbyn Ffrainc fel y gwelwn y chwaraewyr yn newid o'r crysau coch i siaced giniawa a thei ddu ar gyfer cinio swyddogol a dathlu.

Mae *Inside The Camp: Wales Grand Slam 2012* yn talu teyrnged i ymroddiad a dyhead pawb yn gysylltiedig â chyflawniadau'n harwyr rygbi. Bydded i fwy o lawer o benodau gael eu hysgrifennu yn y blynyddoedd i ddod.

2011 RUGBY WORLD CUP

Wales get ready for the fray

Expectations for the RBS 6 Nations tournament in Wales were high after Warren Gatland's team had deservedly reached the semi-finals of the Rugby World Cup in New Zealand a few short months earlier.

In many ways Wales had become a pivotal story of the competition in 2011 as their performances on the field were balanced by behaviour off the field which won the hearts and minds of the rugby world.

The work ethic of the squad and the intensity of the preparation before and during the Rugby World Cup showed that this young team was afraid of nobody.

They lived, ate and breathed rugby with a devotion to excellence which translated into supreme confidence during each and every game.

They were halted in their progress by a powerful France unit which went on to test the All Blacks to the limit in a closely-fought final.

When that game was being played, the Welsh squad was already heading in to land at Heathrow Airport to the adulation of a nation which had seen its rugby pride restored.

The team had been shocked and delighted to learn that some 60,000 fans had packed the Millennium Stadium back home to watch a big screen broadcast of their semi-final encounter against France.

Every player and coach involved in the senior Welsh squad knows that the RBS 6 Nations tournament is one of the toughest and most unpredictable there is.

But after the lessons of Rugby World Cup 2011, Wales were ready for anything.

The World Cup campaign is about to get underway with a thrilling encounter with defending champions South Africa

The win over Samoa gave Wales real momentum

WATER

Lee Byrne scores one of 12 tries accumulated against Namibia

Scott Williams flies over the line in the demolition of Fiji

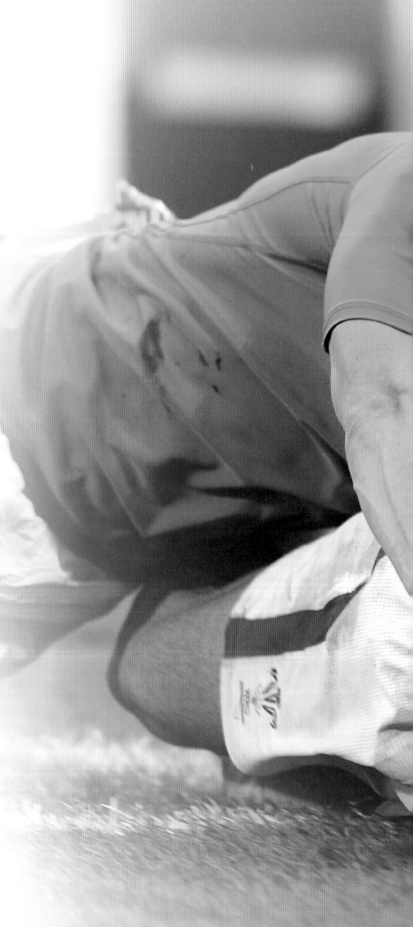

COME ON WALES!

Wales fans showed why some call them the world's best

It is almost certainly unprecedented for 60,000 fans to pack a rugby stadium to watch the live screen broadcast of a match being played 12,000 miles away.

When it happened at the Millennium Stadium in Cardiff, when Wales were playing France at Eden Park in Auckland, New Zealand, the event was reported worldwide as a rugby phenomenon.

By 9am on a crisp Cardiff morning, excited fans were streaming into their beloved stadium to soak up the surreal atmosphere.

In New Zealand, the Welsh team was well aware of the astonishing turn-out and the coaches were happy for that knowledge to help inspire their performance.

In Wales, a nation woke up to the reality that rugby truly is its national sport and touches the hearts and minds of the people from communities up and down the land.

The recognition of the Welsh effect was sensed in London's Downing Street where a Red Dragon flag was flown in honour of the team and their achievements.

In the stadium itself, the bowl of the ground where the matches are played out became a sea of red as fans stood shoulder to shoulder and roared their admiration for Sam Warburton's warriors.

More people watched the semi-final on big screens at the Millennium Stadium than were present at the actual match at Eden Park, Auckland

Toby Faletau on the charge in the World Cup semi-final

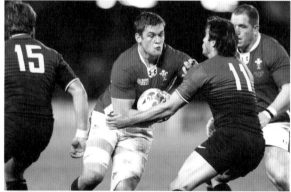

Wales so close as France edge win

The semi-final clash between Wales and France at Eden Park in Auckland will inevitably stir memories of a red card handed to the Welsh skipper Sam Warburton.

It caused a controversy, but for Sam and the Wales camp, there were no complaints.

Wales scored the only try but eventually went down by one point in a 9-8 finish which ended hopes of a World Cup shock.

The third place play-off against Australia also proved a match too far, but the final score of 21-18 to Australia proved to one and all that Wales are true contenders at this level of the modern game.

Perhaps a crucial factor in the two lost games is that Wales never gave up in either and were contenders until the final whistles were blown.

Warren Gatland wanted to create a team which no side could take their foot off the pedal against. With this Wales team, his ambition has surely been realised.

The players salute the fans after a heartbreaking one-point defeat to France

POLE POSITION

Polish preparation gives
Wales ice cold determination

Wales prepared for the RBS 6 Nations tournament by returning to Poland for a gruelling schedule of training sessions.

The run-outs were interspersed with time in the cryogenic chambers which freeze away the aches and pains of hard training.

The 'fridge' sessions allowed muscles to repair quickly so the coaches could pack more meaningful work into a short space of time in order to get the squad into the precise shape they wanted them. Of course, the lack of frills or temptations in the camp near Gdansk also served to forge powerful bonds between players who were away from the familiar luxuries of life in top class hotels.

The snow lay thick on the ground where the team run-outs took place in between those ice chamber sessions where temperatures plummeted to 130 degrees Fahrenheit below freezing point.

The Polish visit took place at a point around midway through the domestic rugby season so the tired limbs of players needed to be nursed back to a physical peak.

The first opponents were Ireland in Dublin, so there would be no gentle entry into the 2012 competition.

The squad returned to their base at the WRU National Centre of Excellence in the Vale of Glamorgan ready to focus on detailed preparation for the first game of the tournament.

Relaxation ahead of the rigours of the training camp

George North takes
aim with a snowball

The players did not go to Poland to stay in luxury, as Leigh Halfpenny's spartan room demonstrates

Down to business

Every member of the squad knows that the job entails absorbing an enormous amount of relevant information.

Nothing is left to chance and the coaches and conditioners make sure the players fully understand every aspect of their preparation and match planning.

For the Head of Physical Performance, Adam Beard, that means staying closely in touch with the players throughout the year.

Any individual in contention for international honours must be monitored and helped to improve.

The camp objectives are clearly set out by Adam so that everyone knows exactly what to expect and what is expected of them.

Pondering what lies ahead

Lee Byrne treads a chilly path in Poland where the
reality of life as a Welsh international rugby player is
probably far removed from the image the public have
of their lifestyles.

This is a working environment and the boys know
they are being tested and measured both physically and
mentally by the coaching staff.

Warren Gatland constantly reminds them of what
an honour it is to be handed the Welsh jersey and that
privilege comes at a price.

George North's immense strength was key to Wales' successful season

No frills but players have an appetite for success

Food is a vital component of the preparation programme for any international rugby player.

The work achieved in any average training week means they need plenty of the right produce to keep their bodies and minds working properly.

They will be measured for their hydration levels, weight and body fat so there is no room for complacency.

This team is renowned for its strength and fitness and the conditioners focus on every aspect of their daily lives which can affect their status.

Toby Faletau takes the
opportunity to refuel

Indoor sessions are no easy break from the winter chill

Training is a mix of rugby drills and specialised fitness modules to improve all aspects of physical performance.

Luckily for the boys, some of the Poland sessions are held in the indoor facilities away from the biting chill of the winter weather.

Of course that does not mean any let-up in the intensity of what is required. The cryotherapy sessions mean the boys can work harder and harder and harder.

The forwards mean business as
they run through the scrum

Alex Cuthbert demonstrates the
team's commitment to tackling

Sidelined by ankle blow

A forlorn Dan Lydiate sat out the sessions in Poland as a recurrence of his Rugby World Cup ankle injury threatened his Six Nations prospects.

The coaches knew that Dan had already proved he had the mental toughness to knuckle down and focus on getting better. He did it in New Zealand and was about to prove it again at home.

All the players knew that Poland was a stage on which to impress the senior coaches with your skills, determination and resilience.

There was no doubt about Dan's determination and importance to the team and he was going to prove just what it takes to be a winner at this ultimate level of the game.

Dan Lydiate's ankle injury ruled him out of the opening fixture against Ireland but he still went on to be named Player of the Tournament

Players must stay in the swim

Players recuperate in the pool easing muscles into action after some of the intensity of Poland.

This is a regular form of exercise and plays an important part in the care and maintenance of hard working bodies.

So many aspects of their lives are competitive, but the smiles show that a session in the swimming pool can also prove a welcome diversion.

47

The players prepare to enter the extreme cold of the cryotherapy chamber at the Polish Olympic training centre

The hurting helps

It's pretty tough. In Spala it's a bit more modern than the camp we went to before the World Cup and the training is very individualised depending on the needs of different players.

Before the World Cup, Poland was very much a pre-season environment, but now midway through the season, boys have different needs.

Some are nursing niggles, so part of the week may involve some recovery and then more intense work later on.

The boys reaped the rewards of the last camp and this is the same. We are going into a competition against some very good rugby teams especially with Ireland first up away from home.

We have got no illusions about just how tough it is going to be, so part of the time in Poland is about the mental focus required.

– Jamie Roberts

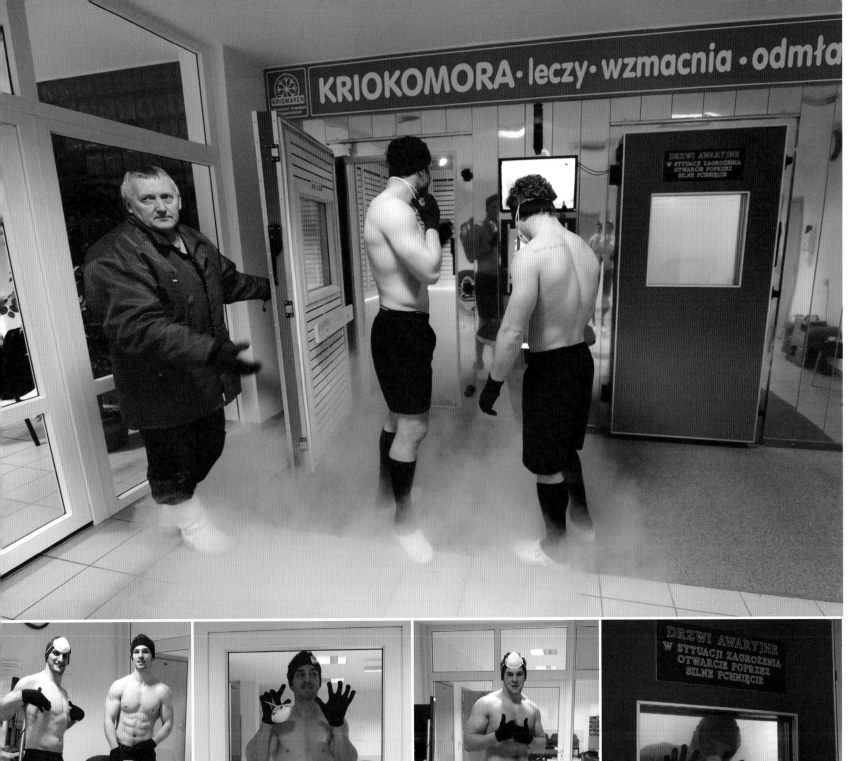

The hard work is about to start as the squad arrives on an icy beach

The beach proves an ice breaker for squad morale

"There were times in Poland when you were at your lowest, physically and mentally. It was so cold there that when we trained on the beach, it was covered in snow.

Your mind becomes drained and you need the support of your team-mates to pull you through and make sure you all get to the finishing line together.

There were no home comforts during our time in Poland: the rooms were basic, no nice beds and the food was not to our taste, as there was egg with everything. No-one there spoke our language.

It was a hard environment, like a military camp. You were pushed to breaking point.

There were times when you felt like giving up but you knew you had to pull through and, from somewhere, you found an extra bit."

– Leigh Halfpenny

Curious Polish people look on as the players stop for a breather

Adam Jones leads back a tired group after a strenuous training session on the beach

Warm praise for Poland

One of the key things about being out here in Poland is that we are able to concentrate on our rugby preparations 24 hours a day.

There are no distractions out here and, personally, I know that going to Spala last year made a definite positive impact on me physically and there is also a psychological impact.

There's no magic wand, the 'cryo' would be no good without the hard work either side of it. We won't know if what we have done here has had an effect until we play, but success at international level is about very small margins and we know we are giving ourselves the best chance by working hard.

– Huw Bennett

RBS
6 NATIONS
CHAMPIONSHIP
2012

LIGHTS CAMERA ACTION

Smile please: You are in the Wales squad

The traditional squad photo shoot is a signal that much of the hard work is already done and the team is ready for action.

It's a moment of light-hearted camaraderie when there is time for a laugh and a joke away from the focus of RBS 6 Nations preparations.

Each Wales squad now poses for this photograph outside the WRU National Centre of Excellence in the Vale Resort where they are based.

The coaches know the importance of bonding as a squad and the environment around the team room at the NCE allows them to chill out in groups.

Before this tournament, the boys were asked to pose for another squad photograph wearing the jerseys of the Principality Premiership Division they first represented.

They are all particularly proud of their rugby roots and it was an opportunity they embraced enthusiastically.

Players change into the colours of club and country as they get ready for the pre-6 Nations photo shoot

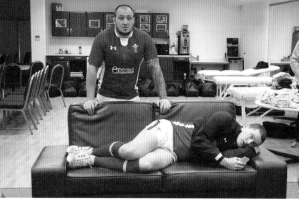

Those sitting down had to carry their own chairs!

Men of Wales

The players show their Principality
Premiership club colours, too

FLYING START

Ireland will prove a tough first encounter

Wales were labelled underdogs in the final build-up to the opening RBS 6 Nations encounter in Dublin because of a crop of injuries to pivotal players.

Gethin Jenkins, Matthew Rees, Dan Lydiate and the World Cup lock pairing of Alun Wyn Jones and Luke Charteris were all sidelined.

But inside the camp, Welsh confidence was high as the spirit which blossomed at the Rugby World Cup empowered those fit and available for selection.

Wales had beaten Ireland in the quarter-finals of the World Cup and notched up a win in the last encounter before that, but it all meant the proud men in green would be out for revenge.

The Welsh would be travelling to Dublin for the game and the Aviva Stadium packed with Irish fans is no place for the faint-hearted.

Preparations are fine tuned behind closed doors

The modern rugby player leaves nothing to chance and every aspect of their preparation is monitored by expert coaches and conditioners.

All the training drills are geared to help the players prepare for the rigours of the modern professional game and that means working specific muscle sets for strength and stamina.

Match drills are practised to build on the Welsh strengths and counter the threat of the opponents about to be faced.

For a player to be ready, it means measuring your weight and even your mood each day to show the coaches whether you are the man for the job come selection.

Gatland: We are ready

"We have been working hard, and we feel we are approaching this match with the right attitude and with some good preparation work done.

We are two sides who know each other well. Ireland will not have enjoyed losing to us in New Zealand.

They will want to redress the balance in Dublin, but they will find us in just as determined a mood."

– *Warren Gatland*

Jelly Tots provide a burst of energy (and a sweet taste) for the captain

Wales hungry for success

Wales captain Sam Warburton can afford to replace the energy he loses during a gruelling training session with a sweet treat.

He is a man who lives and breathes his rugby preparation and his matchday performances are testimony to an astonishing level of fitness.

The entire squad knows the intensity of the training ground means they cannot afford to turn up unprepared.

Coaches look closely at every aspect of performance on the training paddock and all the squad want to impress.

At the WRU National Centre of Excellence, the team enjoys some of the best training facilities in the game and when the weather is good, maybe the work doesn't feel quite so hard.

The squad heads to Dublin for the opening game of the 2012 RBS 6 Nations

We are on our way

All the Welsh team travel is organised by WRU executive Lena Rann and her team who know the squad requires smooth transit to and from matches.

Team Manager Alan Phillips oversees arrangements on the day and the players just have to be there on time and ready to go.

As professional players, they are well used to hopping from nation to nation for their regions or with Wales.

The game is fast approaching and they are raring to go, but this is a time to keep calm and relaxed before the hard work ahead.

The Aviva Stadium provides a striking backdrop as Rhys Priestland finds his range in pre-match training

The dressing room is ready: the game is near

Home or away, the Wales dressing room is a place only the privileged few get to see on matchday.

Hours before kick-off, the backroom team arrives at the stadium to make sure everything is prepared for the players.

Each changing area is dressed with the name of the player or reserve and the warm-up and playing kit is laid out in order.

Around the corner, the medics, physios and conditioners will have arranged all their equipment ready for the fray to come.

The Team Doctor, Professor John Williams, is one member of the backroom team who spends hours making sure all his supplies are prepared and to hand.

Before the team arrives, the room is a calm oasis deep in the heart of a stadium which is already buzzing with noise and activity as the fans arrive.

All set for a match to remember

Davies celebrates two-try haul

I was really happy with my performance against Ireland. I've done a lot of work over the last few months to try and improve my all-round game.

I've been working on my handling skills, passing accuracy, just to make sure I am comfortable passing off both hands.

Slowly but surely I am getting close to where I want to be as an all-round rugby player.

I've had a lot of personal frustration about my handling skills and my passing accuracy. But I've done a lot of work on my own to make sure I get to the level that's required for Test rugby.

If you are a weak link in a good back-line, you are going to stand out and eventually lose your place. I've gone away and worked hard.

– Jonathan Davies

Jonathan Davies scores his second try of the game

My heart was pounding

"As soon as the penalty was awarded, my heart began to thump. I've had tougher kicks in my time, much tougher, but 30 metres seems an awfully long way when you are in a position to seal an RBS 6 Nations game. My heart was pounding from the moment I put it on the tee, but to see it sailing through the posts was just such a relief.

– Leigh Halfpenny

Bennett bags 50 caps

"It's such an achievement to get your first cap, then your second and third and so on. Then you have a goal to get to double figures, then it's about continuing to play for Wales, but your 50th cap still looks a long way away.

It's probably something I will look back on and savour rather than go into too much at this point.

But now it's come around, it's an achievement I will be very proud of, but there's also that extra incentive to do well because it's your 50th cap.

For me it's all about keeping going. It is an honour to get to 50 but the game is more important than personal honours."

– Huw Bennett

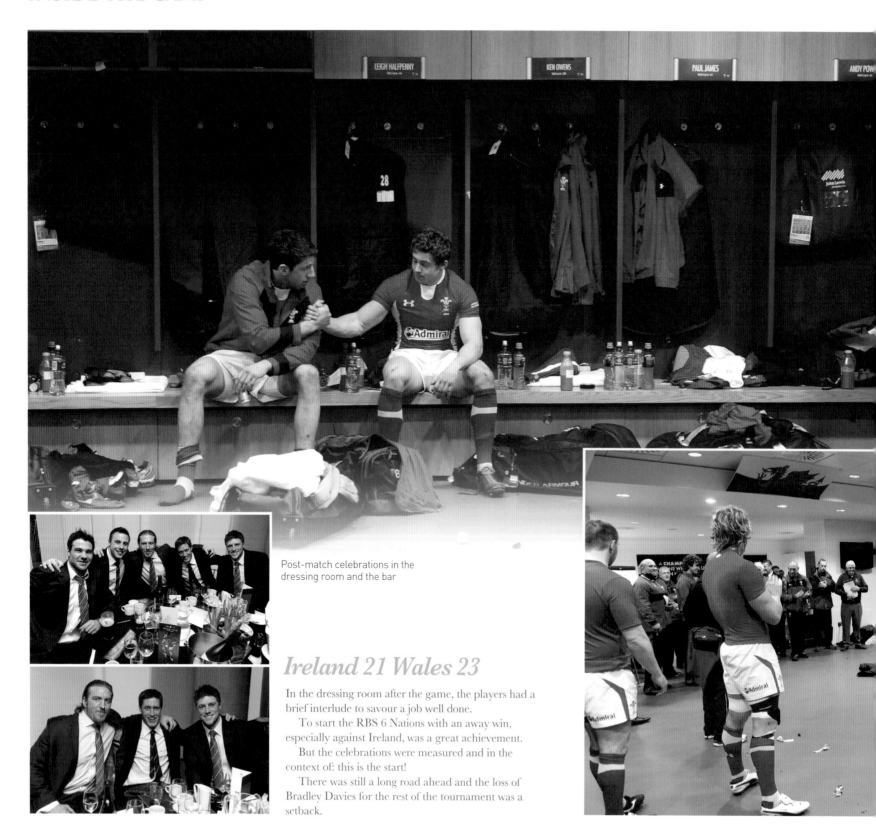

Post-match celebrations in the dressing room and the bar

Ireland 21 Wales 23

In the dressing room after the game, the players had a brief interlude to savour a job well done.

To start the RBS 6 Nations with an away win, especially against Ireland, was a great achievement.

But the celebrations were measured and in the context of: this is the start!

There was still a long road ahead and the loss of Bradley Davies for the rest of the tournament was a setback.

Warren Gatland congratulates his players on a winning start

HOME COMFORT

Wales prepare a warm welcome for the Scots

The Wales squad had no illusions about the task ahead when they prepared to face Scotland at the Millennium Stadium in the second game of the tournament.

Scotland play a brand of rugby which matches the energy levels of any team and the smallest mistake will be punished.

The athleticism of the Scots was epitomised in their starting lock combination with the all-action style of Richie Grey complemented by the hard work and effort of Jim Hamilton.

Wales had injury worries from the start of the week over Sam Warburton's dead leg and Ryan Jones looked set for a second row call-up with the enforced omission of Bradley Davies.

All in all it was far from business as usual, but Wales had been here before with injury worries and the squad depth was now strong.

Some heavy (and not so heavy) weights being lifted in the gym

Players go the extra mile in strength training at the NCE

In the modern era, the professional player allows nothing to chance in his preparation for top class rugby.

Every man in the squad has to be at peak fitness and powerful enough to meet the toughest of challenges for eighty minutes and more.

The Wales squad preparation schedule contains daily doses of gym work where the weights are heavy and the repetitions exhausting.

Most of the sessions take place at the gymnasium on the ground floor of the WRU National Centre of Excellence. Much of the activity is captured on video by the analysts and conditioners so there is no hiding place for players.

Forwards and backs may differ in the specifics of their weights programmes, but whatever position you play for Wales, you will need to match your talent with strength.

Toby Faletau takes a
chance to get some rest

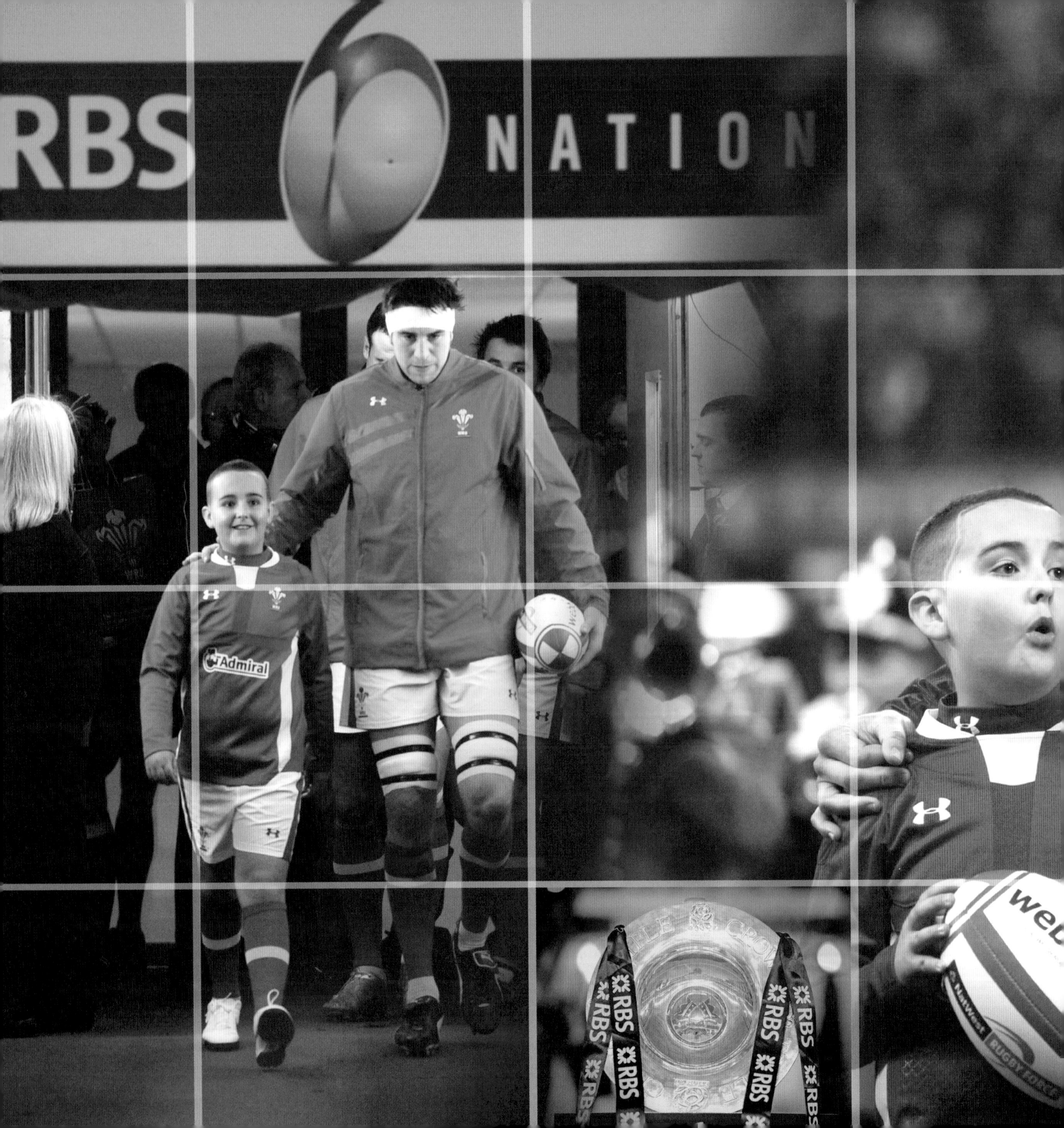
RBS
NATION
Admiral

Delighted to skipper Wales

" It was a fantastic occasion, for myself, my family and
my friends. Equalling Ieuan's record is something
we'll treasure and look back on in years to come.
It's something we never thought I would achieve when I
started out, but as it came closer, it became something that,
like it or not, I did start to strive for.

It's a wonderful accolade to finish my rugby career with,
whenever that may be. It's something in a few years time, or
even in the summer, I can sit back and reflect and have a glass
of wine and have a good laugh and joke about it.

– Ryan Jones "

Alex Cuthbert crosses the line
on his 6 Nations home debut

George North is tackled by Scotland fly-half Greig Laidlaw

Congratulations for Cuthbert after his try

Wales put Scots to the sword

Alex Cuthbert and Leigh Halfpenny scored all the points for Wales to beat Scotland by 27-13 at the Millennium Stadium.

Three tries during an intense 14 minutes of Welsh attacking effort in the second half sealed the fate of the visitors.

Cuthbert crossed for his first for Wales at the Millennium Stadium before Halfpenny grabbed two more. Captain Sam Warburton had been ruled out shortly before kick-off after failing a late fitness test on his dead leg.

Warren Gatland opted to move new boy Aaron Shingler straight in at number 7 and there was universal agreement that he did himself proud.

The importance of the victory was lost on no-one as Wales had set up a Triple Crown showdown at Twickenham.

Leigh Halfpenny scores his second try of the game

93

xxxxxx: caption words to come please

Alex Cuthbert is halted by the Scottish defence

We believed in ourselves

It was a bit of a tale of two halves. We were frustrated with how we went in the first half when for some reason we were a bit panicky when we attacked. We took a couple of poor options and we lost the ball in vital areas as well.

At the interval, there was no rollicking from Warren and the coaches, it was more a case of looking calmly at what we needed to do.

Everyone recognised that if we kept our composure and went through our patterns and structures, we had the capability to take control of the game, and thankfully we did just that in the second half.

I think not conceding a try right at the end of the first half, when the Scots were coming at us in wave after wave, acted as a massive psychological boost because right from the restart we took a stranglehold.

We deserved it by the end because I felt we worked hard to get through the difficult patches. I'd be lying if I said it wasn't a bit nervy at 3-3, but these days there is strong self-belief in the squad that can get us through in tight situations.

– Leigh Halfpenny

Leigh Halfpenny applauds the supporters after the final whistle

Rhys Priestland reaches out to the home support as he heads for the tunnel

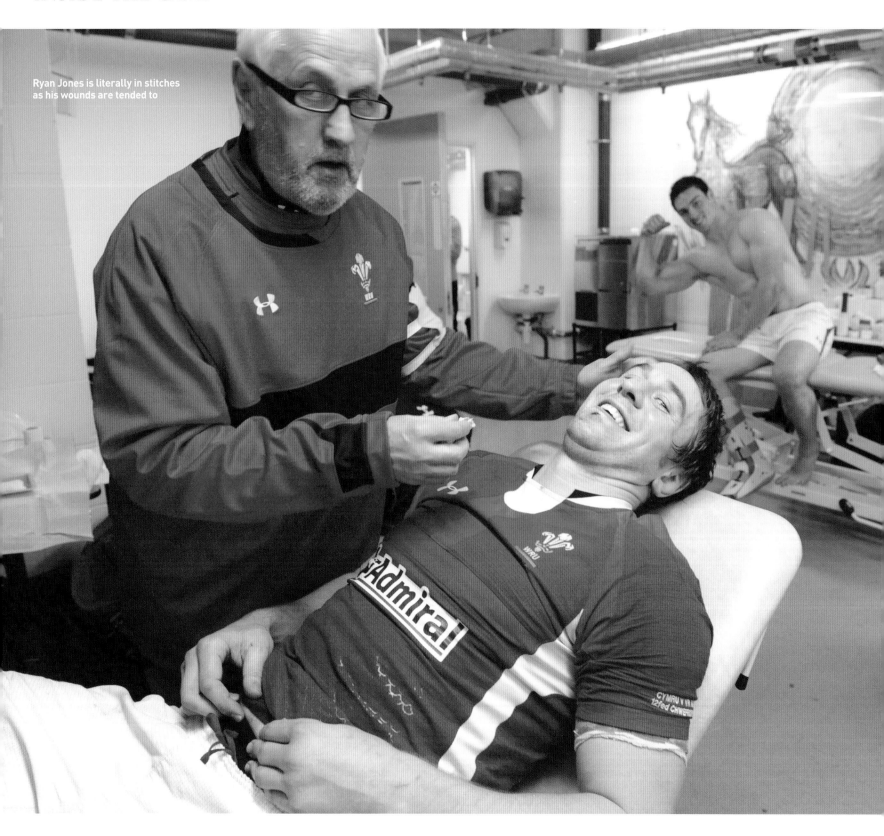

Ryan Jones is literally in stitches as his wounds are tended to

CROWN JEWELS

Great Scott is Welsh super sub at Twickenham

Writing your name into Welsh rugby folklore is something very few have the talent and determination to achieve.

Scott Williams entered the fray from the bench against England and did just that with an astonishing second half try.

They say you make your own luck and Williams ripped the ball from a maul in a drill practised time and time again on the training paddock.

This time it was for real and the young Scarlet could not hide the delight on his face as he dived over at the posts.

This was England: it was HQ and victory would secure a Triple Crown for Wales.

Captain Sam Warburton was able to return for Wales so the World Cup back row trio of Lydiate, Faletau and Warburton was back together.

It was not to prove an easy encounter as England gave their all right up until the dying moments of the match.

Moves are practised on the training pitch, while, in the bottom pictures, Ryan Jones attempts to lock Dan Lydiate in the portable toilet

There could be no let-up as the ultimate prize came nearer

Welsh players and coaches are well aware of how the expectations of a nation can rise dramatically during a winning streak for Wales.

As the fans savour the scent of victory, the squad knows full well that the reality of the situation is quite different.

England are a formidable outfit and the training had to be spot on if Wales were to stand any sort of chance in front of more than 80,000 spectators at Twickenham.

The squad travelled to London late in the week and, as usual, kept the training ground away from prying eyes.

This was a Welsh squad determined to reap the rewards of all their hard work and the Crown was tantalisingly close.

Only an honoured few get a seat on the team bus

The team bus is a special environment which the players and coaches guard as a sanctuary for their quieter moments of togetherness.

When the games are over the horizon, it can be a place for banter and chat after or before training sessions.

But on matchday, it is a place where you can cut the atmosphere with a knife.

Back home in Wales the players and coaches are constantly amazed by the huge welcome they are given by the home fans as they head into Westgate Street and the Millennium Stadium's Gate 4.

Here in London, the onlookers are slightly more muted, but the Welsh are still there and the familiar coach is spotted by those in the know.

For some players, it is a time for quiet reflection, others tune in to their favourite music. All of them know they face an exhausting battle ahead.

Gethin Jenkins has his serious face on

A band of brothers

Line-out routines are practised ahead of the England match

Friends amongst the rugby foes as the match looms

The Welsh squad turned up at the Wasps training ground for one of their final sessions before taking on England at Twickenham.

The relaxed atmosphere was helped by catching up with some old friends who now ply their rugby trade in the UK capital.

As Director of Rugby at London Wasps, David Young turned up to meet his many old friends from Wales.

For Rob Howley, Warren Gatland and Shaun Edwards, Wasps is familiar territory and they know the training facilities well.

Another Welsh newcomer to London is Tom Prydie who shared a quiet chat with his former Ospreys team-mate Ryan Jones.

The Welsh boys felt at home: was that just luck or yet another piece of the pre-match jigsaw put together by the coaches who mastermind Welsh success?

Arm in arm and ready to go

Triple Crown joy for Wales

Captain Sam Warburton turned in a man of the match performance and summed up the feelings of his team-mates after accepting the trophy.

He said: "Lifting the Triple Crown was probably the best moment of my career so far. It shows all the hard work we've put in over the last 12 months has paid off. We've got some recognition now and a little bit of silverware."

Of course it wasn't easy as England stayed in the game all the way before Wales welcomed the final whistle at 19 points to 12.

Four penalities apiece from Halfpenny and Owen Farrell had locked the scores at 12-all.

It was then that Scott Williams decided to act out every schoolboy's dream by grabbing the ball to score the winning try for Wales.

There was drama at the end when David Strettle got close to scoring, but after several minutes' deliberation, the television match official ruled no try.

Wales had secured their 20th Triple Crown in a game oozing drama.

Mike Phillips tries to break through the English ranks

Leigh Halfpenny finds the target

Dan Lydiate carries
the fight to England

Scott Williams dives over for
the match-winning score

Diving head first into history

It's quite unbelievable. The try happened so fast and I can't really remember what I was thinking. There was a bit of luck with the bounce, but I had a feeling it was going to pop up and it went straight into my hands.

– Scott Williams

Satisfaction following a superb victory at Twickenham

Gatland: This team will get even better

 I said to the players before the game, they had a chance to create history. They've done that, and I'm delighted.

It was a great Test match. England's defence was excellent. Maybe the occasion got to some of our younger players; Leigh Halfpenny missing his first kick and maybe Rhys Priestland did not have his best game, but he came through that.

We showed signs of great composure and character, that's a sign of a team which will get better in time.

– *Warren Gatland*

The tension is released after the video referee decided England have not scored a last-minute try that could have levelled the score

Sam Warburton holds aloft
the Triple Crown shield

We dug deep to win

England did extremely well. They came out with a real edge about them and were very physical.

But the boys dug in deep for each other and came out the other end.

I couldn't believe it after the game – I just kept screaming 'Triple Crown'.

– Jonathan Davies

Ian Evans finds an unusual use for the Triple Crown shield

George North was hungry for silverware

Twickenham silverware

Three games in you don't normally have a bit of silverware under your belt.

It was nice to toss it round the changing room after the game. It's a big trophy to win.

There were a lot of happy people in the dressing room and probably a lot more happier in Wales.

We've won the Triple Crown in Twickenham. We've never done that before. It's a big scalp beating all the home nations. It's also nice that we've got the two last games at home.

— *Gethin Jenkins*

Toby savours victory

When I look back over the past couple of years, things have moved so fast. There have already been a few highlights, with the World Cup in New Zealand a major thing for me. Playing with the boys and learning so much off the guys is a great experience. Then to go on and win the Triple Crown and Grand Slam was awesome. And to have the best fans in the world following us is great. Walking around seeing all the Welsh flags waving at Twickenham was amazing.

– Toby Faletau

Skipper Sam gets his hands on the silverware

Lifting the Triple Crown was probably the best moment of my career so far. It shows all the hard work we've put in over the last twelve months has paid off. We've got some recognition now and a little bit of silverware.

— *Sam Warburton*

THE ITALIAN JOB

Wales march on against a brave Italy

The Triple Crown winners had it all to lose when Italy arrived in Cardiff with a mission to block their route to the Grand Slam.

Wales knew of old how the Azzurri could cause upsets against the biggest teams around.

The fans may have been oozing confidence for Wales, but the squad knew that any let-up in intensity would be punished.

It would need a performance up to the usual intensity and a realisation that the Italian defence would be tough to crack.

In the end, Wales achieved their goal by sticking to their task to eventually carve gaps through the assured Italian tacklers.

It ended 24 points to 3 for Wales and the Dragon was still breathing fire.

You have to train hard to win!

The build-up to the Italian encounter lacked none of the intensity of all the other RBS 6 Nations encounters.

Every player knew that the coaches were monitoring their every move and the competition for places was as strong as ever.

The build-up followed a pattern the Wales squad players are now familiar with and their professionalism and personal pride shines through every session.

Of course there is time for a joke and a laugh, but when the time arrives for the work to start, then the focus is one hundred per cent.

Rhys Priestland strains to lift a heavy weight

Back at the Millennium Stadium
for the final two fixtures

Pride in the jersey

In the 2012 competition, Wales faced all three of the 'Blues teams in Cardiff with Italy the second home game of the tournament.

Italy boast some of the world's best players with the number eight and skipper Sergio Parisse a household name in rugby circles.

The Welsh players have total respect for the opposition and the pride in the jersey is colossal as they enter the matchday routine.

In a tantalising gesture, the Grand Slam trophy is on show at pitchside as the fans start to fill the stadium.

Roberts and Cuthbert grab the tries for Wales

Wales displayed their patience against a stern Italian defence throughout the first half with Leigh Halfpenny grabbing all nine Welsh points with his boot.

The 9-3 interval lead was extended with tries from the Blues pair of Jamie Roberts and then Alex Cuthbert.

Roberts had to race 60 metres for his touchdown and then three minutes from time, Man of the Match Cuthbert was on hand after prop Gethin Jenkins fed the ball from a quick tap penalty.

A Priestland penalty completed Wales' unanswered 15-point second half tally.

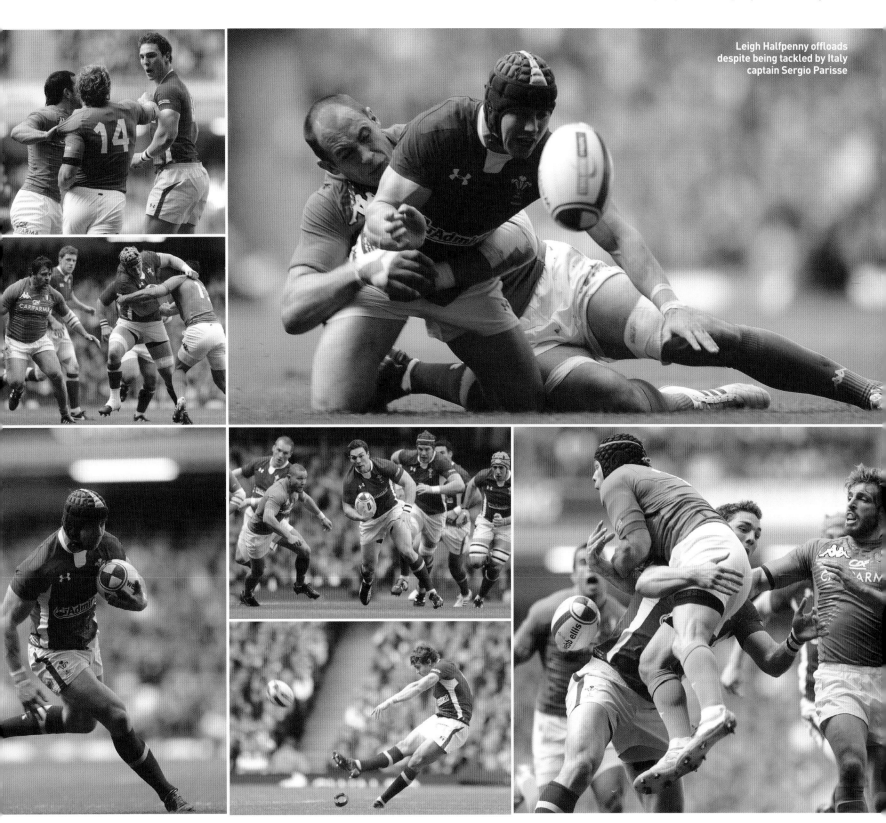

Leigh Halfpenny offloads despite being tackled by Italy captain Sergio Parisse

Jamie Roberts
celebrates his try

Relief all round as Wales win well

> We are just taking each game as it comes. We knew it was going to be tough from the start. Their workrate was outstanding. It was hard to break them down, but we knew if we worked hard, we'd grind them down for a win.

– Alex Cuthbert

Post-match sandwiches for the players to replace the calories they have burnt off

GRAND FINALE

A day of destiny awaited Wales at their stadium

The Millennium Stadium was jam-packed, the streets of Cardiff were full and the whole of Wales was glued to the nearest TV screen.

Wales was hungry for a Grand Slam victory and it was virtually impossible for latecomers to get their hands on a ticket.

The build-up week had been as intense as it can get with the media already scenting the Grand Slam headlines they wanted.

The Welsh rugby legend Mervyn Davies passed away on the eve of the game and his loss was a poignant presence within the squad and around the rugby world.

It was vital for the players to retain their focus and train with the usual intensity as the rest of Wales bathed in the expectation of euphoria.

Warren Gatland's mantra of honesty, hard work and character was to be tested to the full in the cauldron of the Welsh capital.

The famous roof of the stadium was to remain open because of a request from France and there was a deluge before kick-off.

Alex Cuthbert was to emerge as a try-scoring hero to cap a tournament which had marked his arrival at the top of the Welsh game.

Wales as a team were about to deliver on the promise so evident at the Rugby World Cup.

Craig Mitchell and Ryan
Bevington strain as they
attempt to lift a giant tyre

More fun and games
with heavy objects

The harder they work, the luckier they get!

It may be a Grand Slam decider but the pain in every players' muscles feels exactly the same during those build-up sessions.

The coaches want them to be at their best and they also want them to retain focus on the game itself and the importance of their own performances.

Now is the time for the squad to prove its professional maturity and the effort had to be uncompromising in each and every session.

The pattern was unchanged and the intensity was the same, but the prize at the end of all the effort was to be huge.

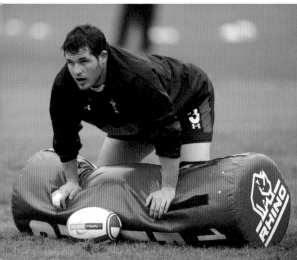

Ready to make history

Home crowd is worth seven points to us

We have experience and the new kids on the block, and it is important we go out and play without fear. Every game you play for Wales as a youngster – and we've got a fair number of youngsters – you become more mature.

They haven't got that baggage of losing games, and through that confidence of the World Cup, we've gained a hell of a lot.

The one thing that is special about this side is that they find a way. In the last 15 minutes of a match, you expect them to go on and win the game.

That mental toughness has sometimes been lacking in previous sides throughout the last couple of decades.

We back ourselves in dogged situations. There will be times we have to dig in and dog it out, and this team finds a way to go and win.

Don't underestimate the influence of the Welsh support. In 2008, coming into this stadium, the support in the streets, the singing, the clapping, for me it just makes the hairs stand on the back of your neck.

I've always said the crowd is worth seven points to the home side. I am sure the players are looking forward to playing in front of the best supporters in world rugby.

– Rob Howley

Players line up for the national anthem in front of their proud fans

Grand Slam dream come true for try ace Cuthbert

"Two months ago I was just expecting to be training with the Blues, not scoring a try in the Grand Slam game.

The players have worked incredibly hard. We've got an awesome group, but I still think we have got a lot more to give as a team and a back-line.

For my try, we got quick ball and I just saw the space and stepped in. Luckily, their full-back Clement Poitrenaud slipped and I just ran through to the line.

It was an indescribable moment, one I will never forget. I didn't know what to do. Maybe it will sink in over the next couple of weeks and I will think about what's going on.

It was an awesome achievement to win the Six Nations and, with the young players we've got, the future is going to be bright.

We're looking forward to the summer tour of Australia. Hopefully, I will get selected for that.

We can only go forward. We have still got a lot to develop and learn as a team, but, I think, as the years go by, we're only going to get better."

– Alex Cuthbert

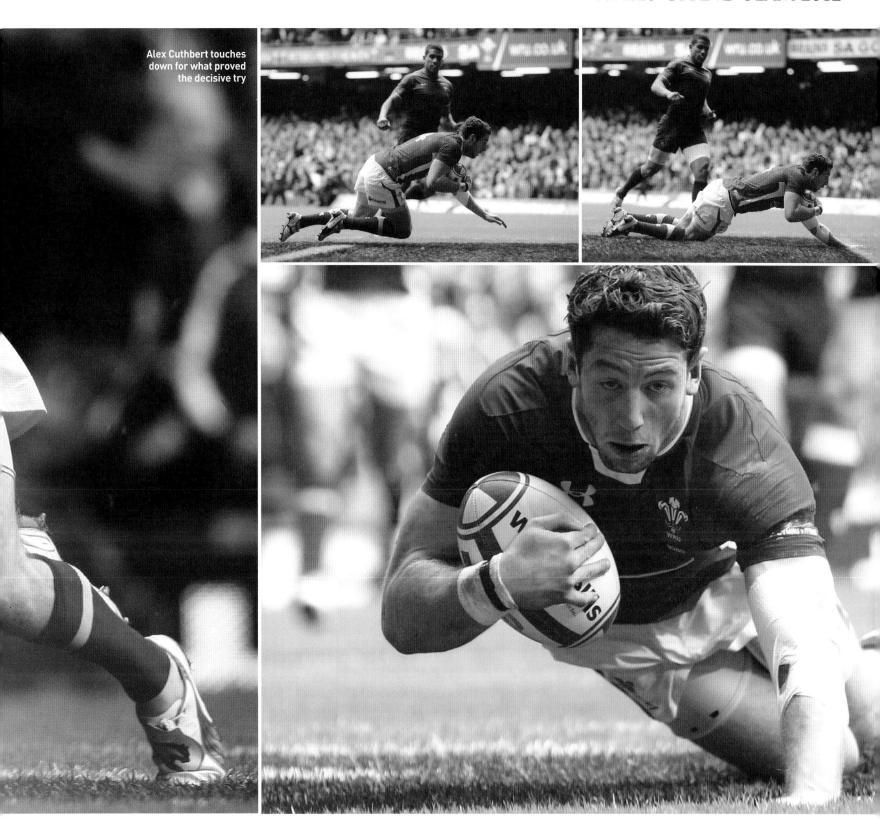

Alex Cuthbert touches down for what proved the decisive try

Cuthbert looks to break free of the French defence

Jones savours his third Grand Slam triumph

It was such a relief at the end, the half hour afterwards, words cannot describe it.

To see my dad and my son in the tunnel as I came off is something I will always remember. And the lap of honour was something else, too. To see people's faces; the joy, perhaps 2012 will become one of those "where were you" moments.

Only time will tell if this side can go on and have sustained success, but this was a different campaign to previous ones. This feels like a more constructed 6 Nations win.

We came in arguably as favourites, or at least as strong contenders, and we were able to convert that and sustain some form.

We had the rub of the green at times, a few bounces of the ball went our way, but that's sport and we managed to convert those into points and claim the five wins.

It's great to feel you have contributed and feel a part of it and I felt I did that. It means you feel you have the right to be there and share it with the guys.

I was way out of my comfort zone at number seven. It is not something I have had experience of, even at regional level really.

I just was able to go out and do my best. I was told to just go and play what I saw, but I don't think Justin Tipuric and Sam have too much to worry about just yet.

It is a great group of guys and the credit needs to go to everyone. We had guys who have trained and not played and people who work in the background, and without those guys we would not have had this success, so it is just reward for the work the guys have put in.

– Ryan Jones

Sam Warburton takes to the podium to hold aloft the RBS 6 Nations trophy

Captain Sam praises his players

I felt a little awkward about going up to receive the 6 Nations Championship trophy, I mentioned this to coach Warren Gatland and asked if he might like to come up with me and lift it together.

He said no immediately. 'It's a player's thing,' he said, 'But if you do feel that awkward, why don't you ask Gethin [Jenkins] and Ryan [Jones] about it?'

Gethin and Ryan had, of course, also been captains during the tournament. I asked them. 'No, it's your moment, you do it,' they both replied. Fair play to them.

It was a superb gesture on both their parts. It certainly made me feel better. And they both still came up to the podium last and stood either side of me.

I absolutely love being involved with the squad we've got at the moment. The relationship between all the players, coaching staff, everything seems to be going well. It was easily the most enjoyable campaign I've been involved with so far and we definitely got our just reward for all the hard work.

– Sam Warburton

The players say a huge thank-you to the Welsh fans

The first people the players wanted to share their triumph with were the loyal Welsh fans.

After the final whistle, they stayed on the pitch for more than ten minutes doing a lap of honour and acknowledging wave after wave of applause.

Some players raised their hands in salute, others clapped their approval of the followers and a few lifted the trophy to show the people what it was all about for them.

After every game the players are drained of energy because playing for Wales demands a workrate few will experience throughout their lives.

But after winning the Grand Slam, Warren Gatland's men each had a skip in their step and a beaming smile on their face.

Bouncing with joy

Jamie Roberts'
headwear turned heads

Smiles and celebrations from the history makers

Only a very privileged few get to see the Grand Slam-winning changing room after the final game has ended and the title has been won.

The job is done for now and everyone can savour the victory and add to the memories of the day.

It is a time for noise and camaraderie when all the aches and pains are temporarily forgotten.

The formalities await and the suits are still on their hangers. Right now it is a time for celebration amongst mates who will remain friends for the rest of their lives.

George North poses with the prize

Toby Faletau shows
the scars of battle

Toby cracks a smile through the pain of victory

The torn jersey bears testimony to the battle fought and won.

Toby Faletau never takes a backward step on the field of play and sometimes that means he goes home wearing the scars of victory.

In game time he is usually found close to the ball and often in a place where others don't want him to be.

Maybe the adrenalin keeps the pain away and after winning a Grand Slam, perhaps the joy of victory is enough to keep it at bay.

Toby's smile is that of a man contented with a job well done. He is not known for seeking out the crowd but everyone knows he is one hundred per cent a team player who will always give his all.

All suited and booted

The splendour of their smart suits stands out against the background of a rugby changing room. No ordinary suits and no ordinary changing room.

This is the Wales changing room and these players have just won the biggest prize in the northern hemisphere international game.

Tonight they don't have to worry about the next international: they have done it, they are Grand Slam winners. Now it is time to savour the moment and make the memories that will last for ever.

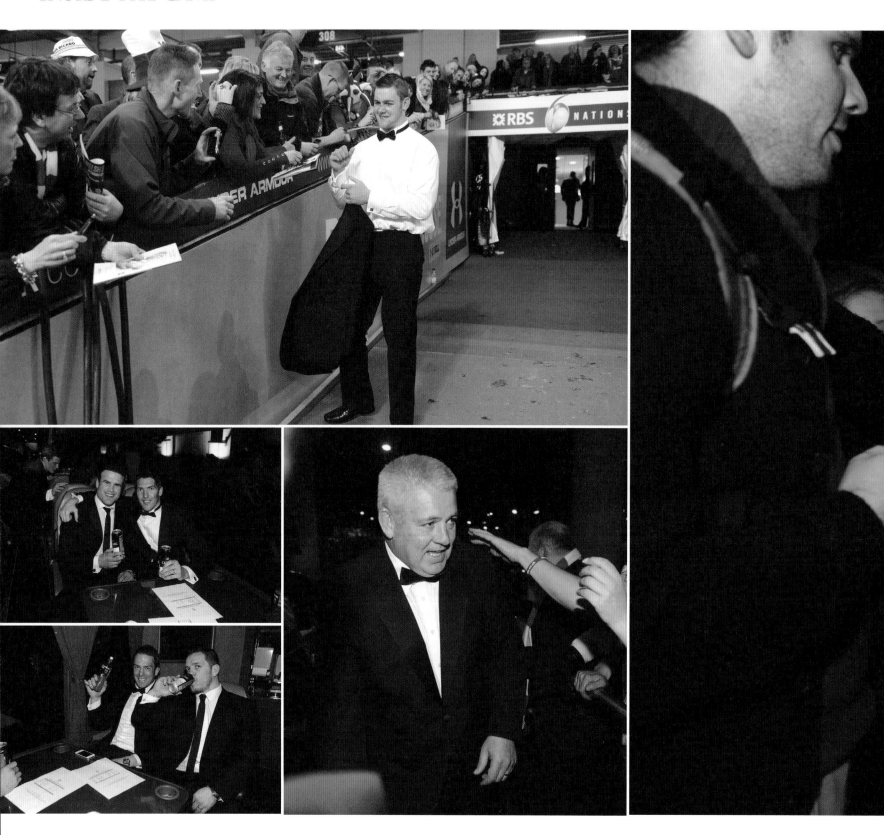

Mike Phillips is showered with acclaim by supporters

50TH CAP

50TH CAP

WWW.UNDERARMOUR.CO.UK

WRU
UNDER ARMOUR
MATTHEW REES
Welsh Cap No. 1033
WRU
1033
50th CAP

UNDER ARMOUR

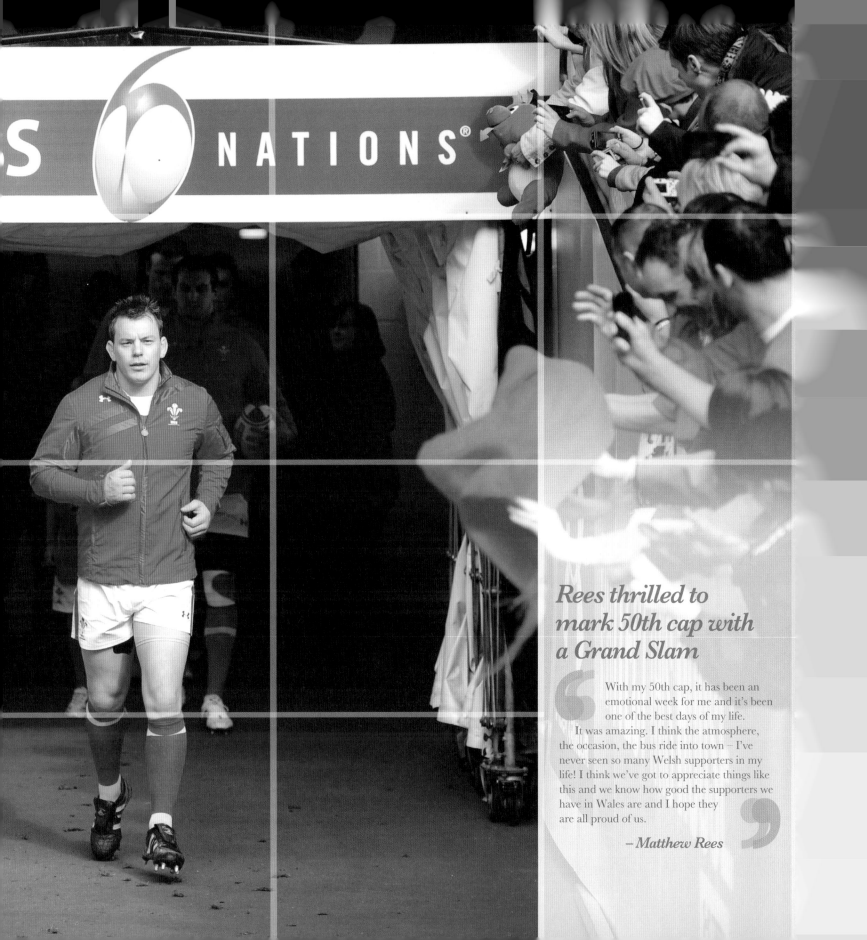

Rees thrilled to mark 50th cap with a Grand Slam

With my 50th cap, it has been an emotional week for me and it's been one of the best days of my life.

It was amazing. I think the atmosphere, the occasion, the bus ride into town – I've never seen so many Welsh supporters in my life! I think we've got to appreciate things like this and we know how good the supporters we have in Wales are and I hope they are all proud of us.

– Matthew Rees

Final words of wisdom

" The last thing I said to them before they
went out on the field was they had a chance
to make the nation proud. They did just
that. These guys have been a real credit to
themselves, to Wales and to Welsh rugby.

— Warren Gatland "

The WRU players and staff share in a glorious achievement

FAN ASSISTANCE

Magnificent support helps propel Wales to glory

Preparation, dedication and inspiration helped Warren Gatland's men achieve the Grand Slam in 2012. The role of the nation's devoted fans should not be underestimated.

They were present, and extremely vocal, every step of the way. The Welsh supporters are undoubtedly the best in the world. This was clearly demonstrated on the day of the World Cup semi-final against France when more people packed the Millennium Stadium to watch on big screens than were in attendance at the actual game in Auckland.

During the RBS 6 Nations, their excitement was tangible; in the streets surrounding the stadiums, and within the grounds too. On the afternoon of the Italy game, the Wales faithful were recorded singing 'Bread of Heaven'. The resulting sound was then released as a single.

After victory over France had clinched the Grand Slam, Gatland paid tribute to the fans, saying: "I thought the crowd were amazing today, particularly in the last few minutes when they got up on their feet and were singing and encouraging the guys to keep hold of the ball."

All eyes on the action

The Scroll Of Honour

Compiled from loyal fans who subscribed to *Inside The Camp*.
They take their place alongside our 2012 Grand Slam heroes

MITCHELL • A JONES • BEVINGTON • G JENKINS
JAMES • GILL • R JONES • REES • BENNETT
OWENS • B DAVIES • EVANS • REED • R JONES
LYDIATE • WARBURTON • TIPURIC • FALETAU
POWELL • M PHILLIPS • L WILLIAMS • WEBB
PRIESTLAND • HOOK • ROBERTS • J DAVIES
S WILLIAMS • HENSON • BYRNE • CUTHBERT • BECK
NORTH • HALFPENNY • L WILLIAMS • HIBBARD
ROBINSON • SHINGLER • S JONES • CHARTERIS
WYN JONES • GATLAND • EDWARDS • HOWLEY
MCBRYDE • A PHILLIPS • N JENKINS • MATHEMA
M DAVIES • RANSON • BEARD • PROF J WILLIAMS
CHAMBERS • BAUGH • ASHBY • LONG • BOWN
HUGHES • ROWLANDS • MORGAN • RICKARD
BATCHELOR • J WILLIAMS • RIMMER • BOSCH

GRANDSLAMS

1908 1909 1911 1950 1952 1971 1976 1978 2005 2008 2012

THE FANS A-B

DONALD ABDUREMAN • HOWARD ABERNETHY • HOWARD ABERNETHY • RANDI ABERNETHY • RANDI ABERNETHY • RACHEL ADAM • BRIONY ADAMS • CHRIS ADAMS • DAVE ADAMS • DAVID ADAMS • DENISE ADAMS • MARY ADAMS • AL • AMY ALCOCK • ANN ALCOCK • GRAHAM ALCOCK • PAUL ALCOCK • TILLY ALCOCK • GERAINT ALEXANDER • JASON ALFORD • KATE ALFORD • ADE ALLEN • BETH ALLEN • DIANE ALLEN • GERAINT ALLEN • KATE ALLEN • MARK ALLEN • NEIL ALLEN • NICOLA ALLEN • SCOTT ALLEN • SOPHIE ALLEN • CHARLOTTE ALLISON • ALUN • AMARAH • EFA GWAWR AMPHLETT-JONES • NERYS AMPHLETT-JONES • BEATRICE ALICE ANDERSON • ELLENOR MAY ANDERSON • HOLLY ANDERSON • KIRTIE GWEN ANDERSON • OWAIN ANDREWS • OWAIN ANDREWS • GARY ANGEL • GLEN ANGEL • ADAM ANGEL FARMER • JEMMA ANGEL FARMER • ESTHER ANGSEESING • FRANKIE ANGUS • JAMES ANGUS • RUBEN ANGUS • SONNY ANGUS • CAROLINE ANKERS • EMRYS ANNE • CIARA ANTHONY • MARK ANTHONY • ED ANTYSZ • FRANCIS DEREK ARCHER • GLENYS ELIZABETH ARCHER • CATHERINE ARNOTT • COLLEEN ARNOTT • JOHN ARNOTT • ALICE ARTHUR • ANNA ARTHUR • ANTHONY ARTHUR • HELEN ARTHUR • RICHARD ASHFORD • ANDREW ASHLEY • CAROLINE ASHLEY • RHIANNON ASHLEY • PATRICK ASTON • NATHAN ATKINS • PAUL ATKINS • RHYS ATKINS-BOND • ANNEMARIE ATKINSON • JADE ATKINSON • KARL ATKINSON • MARK ATKINSON • JEREMY BABER • MIKE BACON • CATHY BAILEY • CHARLEY BAILEY • GEMMA BAILEY • PAUL BAILEY • IESTYN BAIN • SEREN BAIN • CORINNE BAIRD • FRANK BAKER • MARGARET BAKER • MEGAN BAKER • NATASHA BAKER • PETER BAKER • BAMPI • HANNAH BANDY • KIMBERLEY BANDY • PHIL BANDY • ETHAN JOHN BANFIELD • JOHN BANFIELD • JULIE BANFIELD • LOWRI BANFIELD • DEWI BANKS • MEGAN BANKS • NATASHA BANKS • PHILIPPA BANKS • ALUN BANNISTER • EMMA BARBER • DARREN RHYS BARBER • MATTHEW SCOTT BARBER • ANGELA BARCLAY • AGUSTIN BARGIELA • GARETH BARKER • CHRIS BARLOW • NOAH BARNETT • BRENDAN BARRAGO • HUW BARRINGTON • CRAIG BARRY • MARTYN BARRY • RHYS BARRY • HELEN BARTLEY • JULIET BARTLEY • RHETT BARTLEY • TESS BARTLEY • CHARLES BARVLAY • ANNA BASHAM • BEN BASHAM • HOLLY BASHAM • WILLIAM BASHAM • IAN BASKERVILLE • IVAN BASTABLE • CHRISTINE BATES • DAVID BATES • HANNAH BATES • JESSICA BATES • JUDITH BATES • LEANNE BATES • TREVOR BATES • CANHAM BAVERSTOCK • ESTON & CALEB BAVERSTOCK • IEUAN BAVERSTOCK • REBECCA BAVERSTOCK • MIKE BAYNTON • STEVEN BAYNTON • SAM BEACH • HAYLEY ANN BEAUMONT • NEIL BEBBINGTON • BECHLINGER • BECHLINGER • BECHLINGER • BECHLINGER • FREYA BECKER DAVIES • JONATHAN BECKER DAVIES • KIERAN BECKER DAVIES • SAM BECKLEY • MARTIN BEDDOE • GARETH BELL • KATHERINE BELL • GWILYM BELLETT • JOYCE BELLETT • ISOBEL FFION BENNETT • MICHAEL DAVID BENNETT • RACHEL HELEN BENNETT • NICOLA BERBILLION • STEVE BERRIDGE • BETHANY • CIAN BETTS • EFAN BETTS • JANET BETTS • PATRICIA BETTS • STEPHEN BETTS • LOWRI CHRIS BETTY • ANGHARAD GRACE BEVAN • AUSTIN BEVAN • IEUAN EVANS BEVAN • JOANNE BEVAN • KEITH BEVAN • PAT BEVAN • ROBERT BEVAN • SARAH BEVAN • TINA BEVAN • WARREN BEVAN • ALEXANDER J BILLINGHAM • CELYN T BILLINGHAM • JOSH BIRCH • JEMMA BIRKETT • SUE BIRNAGE • ALEXANDRA BISHOP • CATHIE BISHOP • DAVID BISHOP • HELEN BISHOP • JULIE BISHOP • PETER BISHOP • GERAINT BLACKWOOD • CAROL BLAKE • DAVID BLAKE • DEWI BLAKE • IESTYN BLAKE • SIAN BLAKE • TRISTYN BLAKE • JONO BLOWER • JONO BLOWER • JONO BLOWER • KATE BOARD • SHAUN BOLT • DAVID BOND • GILLIAN BOND • RACHEL BOND • EDDIE BOULTER • CERYS BOUSTEAD • DAVID BOUSTEAD • HAYLEY BOUSTEAD • LUC BOUSTEAD • ANGHARAD BOWDEN • DAVID BOWDEN • JULIA BOWDEN • RICHARD BOWDEN • ARTHUR BOWEN • BETH BOWEN • CHRISTOPHER NEVILLE VAUGHAN BOWEN • EMMA CARYS BOWEN • IAN BOWEN • IAN BOWEN • JANETTE BOWEN •

THE FANS B-C

JANETTE BOWEN • NICOLA JANE BOWEN • PAUL GLYNDWR BOWEN • RHIAN BOWEN • RHYS WILLIAM BOWEN • ROBERT DAVID VAUGHAN BOWEN • STEPHEN BOWEN • STEPHEN BOWEN • THOMAS CHRISTOPHER GEORGE BOWEN • THOMAS RHYS BOWEN • DAFYDD BOWEN JONES • ANGHARAD BOWIE • JOHN BOWIE • KATE BOWIE • ALAN BOWKETT • JAMES BOWKETT • JAYNE BOWKETT • RICHARD BOWKETT • JO BRANDON • JO BRANDON • JO BRANDON • BRIAN BRAZIER • RHYS IEUAN BRAZIER • SHARON BREEZE • JACK BRENNAN • VORDEN ANN BRENNAN • CLAIRE BRIDGEMAN • CLAIRE BRIGGS • GARETH BRIGHT • JOEL BRIGHT • MICHAEL BRIGHT • PHIL BRILEY • RACHEL BRILEY • TOMAS BRILEY • TRACEY BRILEY • LOUISE BRITT • THOMAS BRITT • PHIL BRITTON • ROISIN BRITTON • STEVE BROKENSHIRE • BARBARA BROOKS • COLIN BROOKS • SARAH BROOKS • ANDREW BROWN • DANIEL BROWN • DAVID BROWN • GARRY BROWN • GARRY BROWN • JULIA BROWN • PETER BROWN • CHRIS BROWNFIELD • ELLEN BROWNFIELD • RAY BROWNFIELD • SUE BROWNFIELD • OLIVER BRUNE • PETER BRUNTNELL • DANIEL BRYANT • BUKSCHAT • DEBBIE BULL • LAURA BULL • PAUL BULL • DAVID JOHN BUMFORD • MICHAEL PHILLIP BUMFORD • STEVEN DAVID BUMFORD • THOMAS BUMFORD • THOMAS BUMFORD • THOMAS BUMFORD • MOYA BURRAGE • GORDON MICHAEL BURTON • KIAN MICHAEL ALLAN BURTON • KYE MICHAEL ALLAN BURTON • LEE MICHAEL ALLAN BURTON • MISS CHARLYANN BURTON • MR DARRYL BURTON • MR SEAN BURTON • MRS CAROL BURTON • NIGEL JOHN BUSS • GWENNAN BUTLER • JESS BUTLER • OLIVIA KATHRYN BUTLER • CRAIG LEE BUTLER • SUSAN ANNE BUTLER • JOHN ARTHUR BYRD • LEEAH BYWATER • MIKE BYWATER • JOHN CALDERWOOD • DAFYDD CALE • GWEN CALE • HELEN CALE • IWAN CALE • GAYLE CALLAGHAN • IAN CALLAGHAN • SANDRA CALLAGHAN • TONY CALLAGHAN • BRIAN CAMPBELL-BIRD • IRENE CAMPBELL-BIRD • LEE CANTY • CHRIS CARLESS • ELLEN MARY CARPENTER • IAN SKIPPY CARPENTER • MARIA ANN CARPENTER • MARY LOUISE CARPENTER • SARAH ANN CARPENTER • EMILY CARRINGTON • HELEN CARRINGTON • JOHN CARRINGTON • THOMAS CARRINGTON • CASEY • LUKE CAUDREN • LUKE CAUDREN • MORGAN CERRONE • KAI CHALLINOR • EDWARD CHAM • GARY CHAMBERLAIN • PHILIP CHAN • IAN CHAPMAN • ANGELA CHARD • JAMIE CHARD • MICHAEL CHARD • CHARLIE • EDOUARD CHASSEIGNE • LYLIANE CHASSEIGNE • TANZ CHAUHAN • LAURA CHEATLE • RICHARD CHEATLE • SARAH CHEATLE • STEPHEN CHEATLE • JAKE CHESWORTH • RALPH CHESWORTH • JOHN CHIRGWIN • MANON CHIRGWIN • CHRISTOPHER • ANTHONY JOHN CHURCHILL • LIAM JAMES CHURCHILL • ANTHONY JOHN CHURCHILL JNR • ANDY CLARK • HARRY JP CLARK • HARRY JP CLARK • MATTHEW J CLARK • MATTHEW J CLARK • ROGER J CLARK • ROGER J CLARK • SARAH CLARK • WILLIAM J CLARK • WILLIAM J CLARK • LOIS CLARK- • AMY CLARKE • CERYS CLARKE • DARREN CLARKE • DAVID CLARKE • DAVID J CLARKE • IAN J CLARKE • JACK CLARKE • MAIR CLARKE • MARY CLARKE • NIGEL CLARKE • ROSSY CLARKE • JAC CLAY • HEATHER CLEAVER • HEATHER CLEAVER • HEATHER CLEAVER • BEVERLEY CLIFFORD • TERRY CLIFFORD • ROBERT MARC CLINCH • SARAH CLOUGH • ADRIAN COCH • ADRIAN COCH • ADAM COFFMAN • SALLY COLDWELL • SUE COLDWELL • BETHANY COLE • JADE COLE • JAMES COLE • LAURA COLE • LUCY COLE • MICHAEL COLE • MORGAN COLE • TESNI COLE • THOMAS COLE • TONY COLE • GEOFF COLES • GARETH COLLIER • NATHAN COLLIER • SHAUN COLLIER • WENDY COLLIER • CLAIRE COLLINS • GRAHAM COLLINS • LUCY COLLINS • STEFAN COLLINS • STUART COLLINS • ZOE COLLINS • LORNA COLLISSON • LORNA CONNELLY • EMILY CONNOR • DAVID COOK • JAMES COOK • PAULINE COOK • TOBY COOK • CERYS COOKE • DAVID COOKE • MALCOLM COOKE • NORMAN COOKE • PAUL COOKSEY • CHARLIE COOPER • CHARLIE EVAN COOPER • TONY COPPIN • JACK CORDERY • JENNIFER CORFIELD • DAVID CORNFORD • DIANA CORNFORD • JONATHAN CORNFORD • CORNISH • OLIVER CORY • SIMON CORY • SUSAN CORY • WILLIAM CORY • ANGELA COTTRELL • ELLEN COTTRILL • RYAN COTTRILL • STEPHEN COTTRILL • ROSALIND COVERDALE • ASTON MARTIN CRAWLEY •

THE FANS C-E

CHARLES LLOYD CRAWLEY • MICHAEL CREEDON • GARETH CRIPPS-JONES • SIAN CRIPPS-JONES • DAVID CROOK • GEOFF CROOK • KAREN CROOK • MARK CROOK • TRACEY CROOK • JAMES CROSS • ALAN CROSSLEY • ADAM CROZIER • ADAM CROZIER • ANNIE CROZIER • ANNIE CROZIER • ELLA CROZIER • ELLA CROZIER • JOEY CROZIER • JOEY CROZIER • CATHERINE CUBBIN • MEGAN ROSE CUBBIN • PAUL CUBBIN • WILLIAM BILLO CUDDIHY • MICHAEL JOSEPH CUMMINGS • SIAN CUMMINGS • DAWN MARIE CURNOW • TERRY MICHAEL JOHN CURNOW • BRIAN CURTIS • NEIL CURTIS • NICK DACEY • DAD • RHIANNON DALE • TONY DALE • HARRIET DALES • IOAN DALY • KATIE DALY • SEAN DALY • SEREN DALY • MARC DANDO • ALED DANIEL • IEUAN DANIEL • JULIA DANIEL • RICHARD DANIEL • KEVIN KARL DANIELS • ANNE DANKS • VIV DANKS • CHARLIE-JOE-VIZZARD DARBY • ISAAC DAVEY • MARTHA DAVEY • RHODRI DAVEY • DAVID • DAVID • DAVID • JASON DAVIDGE • ADAM DAVIES • ALISON DAVIES • ALISON DAVIES • ANDREW 'DAVO' DAVIES • ANDREW 'DAVO' DAVIES • ANDREW JOHN DAVIES • ANNA-MARIE DAVIES • BEN DAVIES • BETHAN DAVIES • BETHAN DAVIES • CARL RUPERT SCOTT DAVIES • CATHERINE DAVIES • DAVID MORGAN DAVIES • DAVIES DAVIES • DEINIOL DAVIES • DELYTH DAVIES • DORRIEN DAVIES • DYFED LLYR DAVIES • DYLAN DAVIES • EDIE DAVIES • ERNIST JAMES DAVIES • FIONA SIAN DAVIES • FIONA SIAN FRANCIS DAVIES • GARWYN DAVIES • GARY DAVIES • GAVIN DAVIES • GEORGINA DENISE DAVIES • GILLIAN DAVIES • GILLIAN DAVIES • GORONWY DAVIES • GWYNETH DAVIES • HELEN DAVIES • HON GWYN DAVIES • HOWARD DAVIES • IAN DAVIES • IAN DAVIES • IFAN DAVIES • IFAN DAVIES • IOLO PEREDUR GLYN DAVIES • JACK DAVIES • JAMES DAVIES • JENNA DAVIES • JENNA DAVIES • JILL D DAVIES • JO DAVIES • JOEL DAVIES • JOHN DAVIES • JOHN DAVIES • JULIA DAVIES • JULIET DAVIES • KAYLEIGH C DAVIES • KEITH DAVIES • KERI DAVIES • LEWIS DAVIES • LINDA DAVIES • LOUISE DAVIES • LUCY JAYNE HOLT DAVIES • LUKE DAVIES • LYNNE DAVIES • MALI CATRIN DAVIES • MARK E DAVIES • MARTHA DAVIES • MARTHA DAVIES • MARTIN DAVIES • MAUD DAVIES • MEGAN DAVIES • MICHAEL DAVIES • MIKE DAVIES • MIKE DAVIES • MIKE DAVIES • MOLLY DAVIES • MORGAN DAVIES • NICHOLAS DAVIES • NICOLA DAVIES • OLIVER JAI DAVIES • PAUL (POLL) DAVIES • PETE DAVIES • PETER DAVIES • PETER DAVIES • PROF MARTYN DAVIES • RHIANNON DAVIES • RHIANNON DAVIES • ROY DAVIES • RUTH DAVIES • SAMUEL DAVIES • SARA DAVIES • SARAH DAVIES • STEVE DAVIES • STEVE DAVIES • STEVE DAVIES • STEVEN RICHARD DAVIES • SUSAN DAVIES • VERRISS DAVIES • WENDY DAVIES • DAVIES • DAVIES • DAVIES • DAVID GLYN HUW DAVIES • FREDERICK JAMES DAVIES • JENNIFER MARGARET DAVIES • RHYS DAVIES • CHRIS DAVIES • MARK DAVIES-JONES • BAZ DAVIES-WIGLEY • BAZ DAVIES-WIGLEY • JASON DAVIES-WIGLEY • JASON DAVIES-WIGLEY • ALUN DAVIS • AURELIA DAVIS • MARTHA DAVIS • WILLIAM DAVIS-GUY • EVAN JAMES DAY • ADRIAN DEASY • DEET • RENO DE-FEO • ALFIE DENLEY • BETHAN DENLEY • DAVID DENLEY • RHYS DENLEY • ADRIAN DENNEHY • ANDY & MANDY DENNER • BERT DENNER • BETHANY DENNER • RHYS DENNER • JONATHAN DEWEY-HAWKINS • HENRY DILL-RUSSELL • TOM DILL-RUSSELL • COLIN DIMOND • HANNAH DIMOND • NOAH DINGLE • ANN DIXON • IVY DIXON • PAUL DIXON • RICHARD DIXON • VALERIE DIXON • WALTER DIXON • CHRIS DOBSON • ANDREW DODD • JEAN DODD • RON DODD • SARA DODD • SUSAN DODD • GETHIN DONNELLY • JACOB DONNELLY • LEON DONNELLY • TRACY DONNELLY • GREGORY DONOVAN • PAUL DONOVAN • JOANNE DOREY • GILLIAN DOUGLAS (CORLEY) • HORACE DOWDALL • RACHEL DOWDEN • KAREN DOWLER • MICHAEL DOWLER • KATIE DOWNES • ALLAN JOHN DOYLE • LEWIS 'CHEWY' DREW • OLIVER DUNCOMBE-JONES • GARY DUNKLEY • MAXENCE DUPUICH • ALYSON DYER • ADELE EBELING • ERIC EBELING • RACHEL EBELING • SUSAN EBELING • JOSEPH EDEY • TRACEY EDMUNDS • ANGELA EDWARDS • BEN EDWARDS • BETHAN EDWARDS • BRYAN EDWARDS • CELYN EDWARDS • CHRIS EDWARDS • CHRIS EDWARDS • CHRIS EDWARDS • CLAIR M EDWARDS • CLAIR M EDWARDS • DAVID EDWARDS • DAVID J G EDWARDS • DAVID J G EDWARDS • DAVID JOHN EDWARDS • GARETH EDWARDS • GERALD MORGAN EDWARDS • GWYN EDWARDS • IEUAN EDWARDS • JEREMY NEIL EDWARDS • JOHNNY EDWARDS • KATE EDWARDS • KATIE EDWARDS • KELLY EDWARDS • LEE WALES EDWARDS • LUCAS RICHARD EDWARDS • LUCAS RICHARD EDWARDS • LUCY ANN EDWARDS • LUCY ANN EDWARDS • LUCY EMMA EDWARDS • MADISON REECE EDWARDS • MARCIA EDWARDS • PAUL EDWARDS • RHIANNON MAY EDWARDS • RICHARD GARETH EDWARDS • RICHARD GARETH EDWARDS • SHAUN EDWARDS • SIMON EDWARDS • STEVE EDWARDS • SUE EDWARDS • TAYLOR LEE EDWARDS • TERRY EDWARDS • WAYNE EDWARDS • NIA ELIN • NIA ELIN • NICK ELLIOTT • CRAIG ANTHONY ELLIS • FREYA ELLIS • JESSE ELLIS • TAMEZINA ELLIS • LORRAINE ELLIS-WIGLEY • LORRAINE ELLIS-WIGLEY • MADDIE ELLIS-WIGLEY • MADDIE ELLIS-WIGLEY • JERRY ELPHICK • NATHAN ENGLAND • MAIGHAN ESBERGER • AERON EVANS • ALISON EVANS • AMANDA EVANS • ANDREW EVANS • ANDREW EVANS • ANGELA P EVANS • ANWEN EVANS • ASHLEY EVANS • BETHANY EVANS • BRIAN EVANS • CATRIN EVANS • CELIA ROSEMARY EVANS • CLAIRE RHIAN EVANS • CLAIRE RHIAN EVANS • CORRIN EVANS • CRAIG EVANS • DANNY EVANS • DAVID HAYDN EVANS • DAVID JOHN EVANS • DAVID MATTHEW EVANS • DAVID RHODRI EVANS • DAVID WILLIAM EVANS • DELFRYN EVANS • DOMINIC EVANS • DYLAN HUW EVANS • ED EVANS • EDWARD EVANS • ELLIOT EVANS • GARETH A R EVANS • GEOFFREY M EVANS • GLYN EVANS • GLYNDWR DWR EVANS • GWYNDAF ARTHEN EVANS • GWYNN FRANCIS EVANS • GWYNN FRANCIS EVANS • HELEN EVANS • HENRY BELYDDYN WILLIAM EVANS • HOLLY EVANS • IAN JEROME EVANS • IAN RICHARD EVANS • IEUAN EVANS • ISLWYN EVANS • JULIAN EVANS • JULIE RITA EVANS • KEVIN EVANS • KIRSTY EVANS • KYLIE EVANS • LES EVANS • LINDIS EVANS • LLIONS EVANS • LOWRI EVANS • MATTHEW EVANS •

THE FANS E-H

MEIRION EVANS • MICHAEL V EVANS • NICK EVANS • OWEN W EVANS • PAT EVANS • PATRICK GWYN EVANS • PAUL EVANS • PETER EVANS • PETER EVANS • RAY EVANS • RHYS WILLIAM EVANS • ROSS EVANS • STEVE EVANS • SUE EVANS • SUSAN EVANS • SUSAN EVANS • TIFFANY EVANS • WILLIAM ARFON EVANS • EVANS • ROBERT M EVANS • ROGER B EVANS • ANER EVANS BERAZA • DANEL EVANS BERAZA • JESS EVERETT • LOTTIE EVERETT • NOAH EVERETT • EMILY FAFINSKI • STEFAN FAFINSKI • MARK FALCON AND FAMILY • SWINTON FAMILY • SWINTON FAMILY • DAVID FARDY • GARETH FARDY • GAYNOR FARDY • TONY FARDY • PADDY FEATHERSTONE • LIAM FEAVIOUR • GEORGE FERGUSON • IAN FERGUSON • JACK FERGUSON • KAY FERGUSON • CHARLOTTE FERRIS • SIAN FFLUR • CARL OWAIN FIELDING • CARL OWAIN FIELDING • HEATHER FINGERSON • JULIANNE FISH • JULIANNE FISH • SHEILA FISH • SHEILA FISH • ANGHARAD MAIR FISHER • REBECCA NIA FISHER • CAROLE FITZGERALD • FINLAY FITZGERALD • HOLLIE FITZGERALD • BARRY FITZ-GERALD • NAOMI FLEMING • JENNIFER FLETCHER • ROBERT FLETCHER • VICTORIA FLETCHER • ALEXANDER FLOOK • ANDREW FLOOK • KATIE FLOOK • LAURA FLOOK • MARION FLOOK • STEPHEN FLOOK • KATE SOFIA FLOYD • ALLISON FLYNN • ALLISTER FLYNN • CHARLOTTE FLYNN • CHARLOTTE FLYNN • ELIZABETH FLYNN • ELIZABETH FLYNN • JENNIFER FLYNN • KATHLEEN FLYNN • KATHLEEN FLYNN • PATRICK FLYNN • PATRICK FLYNN • SUE FLYNN • TED FLYNN • ANGELA FOLLOWS • DANIEL FOLLOWS • GRACIE FOLLOWS • LYNDON FOLLOWS • CAM FORSYTH • JACK FORSYTH • SHEILA FORSYTH • KIERAN FOSTER • KIERAN FOSTER • RYAN FOSTER • RYAN FOSTER • JAMES BARRIE FOULKES • LEANNE FOULKES • SIMON FOULKES • CERYS FOX • JACK FOX • JOHN FOX • JOHN FOXWELL • ROSS FOXWELL • DAFYDD FRANKLIN • PETER FRANKLIN • JAC FRANKLYN • ANDREW FRENCH • ALI FRIEND • ANNA FRIIS • ANTHONY FRIIS • EVAN FRIIS • MARI FRIIS • ANDREW JAMES FUDGE • ALICIA GARCIA • ALICIA GARCIA • KATIE GARDINER • ANDY GARNETT • BRENDA GARNETT • TOM GARNETT • CAROLINE ANN GARRETT • DEBBIE GARRETT • DYLAN GARRETT • JACK GARRETT • JENNIFER GARRETT • KIRSTY LOUISE GARRETT • LEE ANTONY GARRETT • MAX GARRETT • TREVOR GARRETT • AMANDA GARTON • ANTHONY GARTON • CELYN GARTON • CLARE GARTON • CONNOR GARTON • ELARA GARTON • EVAN GARTON • LEE GARTON • ANN GASH • DYLAN GASH • TOM GASH • GWLADYS GASKIN • MAC GASKIN • GABRIEL GATHERIDGE • GRACE GATHERIDGE • LEIGH GATHERIDGE • LEONNA GATHERIDGE • DAVID GEDRYCH • GEMMA • CERI FRANCES GEMMELL • CHRIS GEMMELL • ANTHONY GEORGE • CAI GEORGE • ELLA GEORGE • JACK GEORGE • KAY GEORGE • NATHAN GEORGE • RHYS GEORGE • ROBERT GEORGE GEORGE • GER • JUDITH GERAGHTY • GRACE EMERY GIBBINS • DARREN GIBBON • GRANT GIBBON • LES GIBBON • TYRON GIBBON • KYLE GILBERT • NANCY GILES • SEB GILES • ZAC GILES • VICTORIA GILL • GARETH GLASS • STUART GLASS • GLENN • HARRI GLOVER • BEN GODDARD • LEAH GODDARD • PETER GODDARD • RACHEL GODDARD • ROY GODDARD • ALEX GODDEN • ALEX GODDEN • AN UNKNOWN GODDEN • DARRYL GODDEN • DARRYL GODDEN • ANDREW GOLDRING • JO GOLDRING • MICHAEL GOLDRING • SUE GOLDRING • AMY GOMEZ • J T GOMEZ • KELVIN F GOMEZ • KAREN GOODALL-LAWRENCE • SAM GOODWIN • TIM GOODWIN • HELEN GORDON • KIRA GORDON • SIAN GORDON • ANN GORE • DAVID GORE • JAC GORTON • NEIL GOSLING • WYN GOWER • CAROL GRAHAM • LES GRAHAM • STEVEN GRAHAM • CARIAD GRAINGER • CARIAD GRAINGER • JAMIE GRANT • JAMIE GRANT • SANDRA GRANT • SANDRA GRANT • SHAUN GRANT • SHAUN GRANT • CHERYL GRAY • STEVEN GREENHALGH • LIZ GREENWAY • MEGAN GREENWAY • OLI GREENWAY • SIMON GREENWAY • EVELYN GREENWOOD • LORNA GREENWOOD • PAMELA GREENWOOD • RAYMOND GREENWOOD • ANNA GREER • JIM GREER • ROB GREER • SIAN GREER • ROBERT GREGORY • STEVE GRENFELL • STEVE GRENFELL • STEVE GRENFELL • ADAM GRIFFIN • DAMIAN GRIFFIN • DOMINIK GRIFFIN • PRISCILLA GRIFFIN • BETHAN R GRIFFITH • SIMON LLOYD GRIFFITH • ALED WYN GRIFFITHS • ALED WYN GRIFFITHS • AMELIA GRIFFITHS • ARTHUR GRIFFITHS • CHERYL GRIFFITHS • COLIN TREASURE GRIFFITHS • COLIN TREASURE GRIFFITHS • COLIN TREASURE GRIFFITHS • COLIN TREASURE GRIFFITHS • DAFYDD JOHN GRIFFITHS • DAFYDD JOHN GRIFFITHS • GLYN GRIFFITHS • IAN GRIFFITHS • JANE GRIFFITHS • JANE GRIFFITHS • KARL GRIFFITHS • OWEN GRIFFITHS • PETER GRIFFITHS • PHILIP GRIFFITHS • SEAN GRIFFITHS • SIAN MARIE GRIFFITHS • SINGUELLA GRIFFITHS • STUART GRIFFITHS • VICTORIA GRIFFITHS • WARD GRIFFITHS • WYN JAMES GRIFFITHS • HUW GRONOW • EINIR GRUFFYDD • BRENT GUARD • WILLIAM GUARD • ANDREA GULLY • CLIVE GULLY • NEIL GUNN • TINA GUNN • MEGAN GUNNING • MIKE GUNNING • BETHAN GUTTRIDGE • JOHN GUTTRIDGE • FERGUS GWALCHMAI • LOGAN GWALCHMAI • NICOLA GWALCHMAI • GWEN • LESLIE GWILLYM • LESLIE GWILLYM • HARRI GWYN • AUDREY GWYTHER • BRYN & PEG GWYTHER • DARREN GWYTHER • SIAN GWYTHER • ALBERT HACKER • CATHERINE HACKER • MARGARET HACKER • STEPHEN HACKER • KAY HAENEY • MANSEL HAENEY • ANDREW HAIGH • COEL MARC HAINES • RHIA FRANCES HAINES • ALAN JOHN HALE • JONATHAN HALE • SYLVIA HALE • WENDY HALE • BRYN OWEN HALL • DUNCAN HALL • TERESA HALL • TOM IWAN HALL • JONATHAN HALSALL • BRIAN HAMBLING • ANN HAMLET • MARY HAMPSON • ROY HAMPSON • JAMES KENNETH HANCOCK • CALLUM HANFORD • TAYLOR HANFORD • JADE HANLEY • CHARLOTTE JOYCE HANSON • MICHAEL GEORGE HANSON • RHYS JOHN HANSON • SAMUEL GEORGE HANSON • LUCAS HARDY • ROB HARES • PAUL HARPER • ROBIN HARRHY • ALLAN HARRIES • ANDREW HARRIES • ANNA HARRIES • ARNOLD HARRIES • GERAINT HARRIES • TOMOS HARRIES • WYN HARRIES • ALEX HARRIS • BETHAN HARRIS • DR ROBERT HARRIS • JAMES HARRIS • JOHN HARRIS • MATTHEW HARRIS • PHIL HARRIS • ROB HARRIS • SUSAN HARRIS • TERENCE G HARRIS •

TERRY HARRIS • TRICIA HARRIS • MORGAN HARRY • MORGAN J HARRY • PAUL HARRY • TERESA HARRY • TERESA HARRY • COLIN HARVEY • EMMA HARVEY • GAVIN HARVEY • MATTHEW HARVEY • GEORGIA LOUISE HARVEY-RICHARDS • MADDI HARVEY-RICHARDS • SARAH LOUISE HARVEY-RICHARDS • ANDY HAWKEN • EMILY HAWKER • EMILY HAWKER • MARK HAWKER • PETE HAWKER • PETE HAWKER • RICHARD HAWKER • VICKI HAWKER • ENZO HAWKER-JONES • ENZO HAWKER-JONES • ANGELA HAWKESFORD • DAVE HAWKINS • RICHARD HAWKINS • RICHARD HAWKINS • SARAH HAWKINS • WENDY HAWKINS • WENDY HAWKINS • STEPHEN HAWTHORNE • TRACEY HAWTHORNE • DAVID HAYES • LYNNETTE HAYES • MEGAN L HAYES • BARRY HEARD • DENISE HEARD • DAVID HEATH • HANAH HEATH • KAREN HEATH • PETER HEATH • RON HEATH • STEVE HEATH • GWENAN HEDD • NEIL HEDGES • CHRIS HELT • MARTIN HELT • GREG HEMBROW • MARIE HEMBROW • NAOMI HEMINGWAY • NAOMI HEMINGWAY • NAOMI HEMINGWAY • BEN HENNESSY • BENJAMIN HENSON • CHARLIE HENSON • DANIEL HENSON • DAVID TAFFY HENTY • CHRIS HERBERT • JAMES HERBERT • NICK HERBERT • RHYS HERBERT • DELWINA HERD • GERTIE HERD • JERRY HERD • MARK HEWSON • GWYN REDVERS HIATT • ALEX HICKS • BRIDIE HICKS • BRYAN HICKS • DAVID HICKS • SUZIE HICKS • JOSHUA HIGBEY • ANDY HIGGS • HELEN HIGGS • JARROD HIGGS • OWEN HIGGS • SAM HIGGS • KATE HIGHY • LAURA HIGHY • LYNNE HIGHY • PHILIP HIGHY • ANN HILL • BECCY HILL • GLYN HILL • GLYNIS HILL • JONATHAN HILL • JONATHAN HILL • KEITH HILL • LAWRENCE AUBREY JAMES HILL • MORGAN HILL • NICK HILL • PAUL HILL • PAULINE SPLEENIE HILL • PETER HILL • PIPPA HILL • RICHARD FROGGY HILL • JACK HINCE • HOGG • KATIE HOLLIDAY • BOB HOLLINGDALE • LIZ HOLLINGDALE • DIANE HOLMES • EDNA HOLMES • JULIA HOLMES • NIGEL HOLMES • THOMAS HOLMES • CLAIRE HOLTON • SAM HONEY • CERI HOPKINS • IONA HOPKINS • JAMES HOPKINS • JO HOPKINS • JOHN HOPKINS • JOHN T HOPKINS • LEE HOPKINS • LLOYD HOPKINS • MARI HOPKINS • NATALIE HOPKINS • NIA HOPKINS • PETE HOPKINS • ROBERT HOPKINS • RUTH V HOPKINS • SARAH HOPKINS • SEREN HOPKINS • MARK HORNER • SHARON HORSINGTON • TIM HORSINGTON • EMILY JADE HOULSTON-JONES • DAVID HOWE • ELISA HOWE • WILLIAM HOWE • ARTHUR WYNNE HOWELL • WILLIAM HOWELL • BETHAN REBECA HOWELLS • BRIAN HOWELLS • BRYN HOWELLS • DAI HOWELLS • DEWI HOWELLS • DREW HOWELLS • GEOFF HOWELLS • JULIA HOWELLS • KEVIN HOWELLS • RHOSYN HOWELLS • BEN HOWLETT • HTHEGOG • ROY HUBBARD • BEN HUGHES • CATRIN HUGHES • CERI HUGHES • GARETH HUGHES • JACKIE HUGHES • JOHN HUGHES • MAC HUGHES • MALCOLM DOUGLAS HUGHES • MEDWYN HUGHES • MEGAN HUGHES • MIKE HUGHES • OWEN HUGHES • STEVE HUGHES • VALERIE HUGHES • HUGHES • BARBARA HULLAH • HAYDN JAMES HULLAH • ROGER HULLAH • WENDY HULME • LINDSAY HULME FLEMING • GARETH HUMBERSTONE • PETER HUMBERSTONE • TERRY HUMBERSTONE • TOM HUMBERSTONE • KENNETH HUME • BETHAN HUNT • BRIONY HUNT • CHRIS HUNT • TRACY HUNT • DANIEL HURFORD • DANIEL HURFORD • JO HURFORD • JO HURFORD • MARC HURFORD • MARC HURFORD • SAM HURFORD • SAM HURFORD • CLARE HURLEY • KATE HURLOW • BETHANY HUTCHINGS • NATALIE HUTCHINGS • SHELLEY HUTCHINGS •RHODRI HUW • DAFYDD HUWS • JULIAN HYDE • IN MEMORY OF PAULINE HAWKINS • RICHARD INCE • PAUL INGRAM • PETER INGRAM • ROSS INGRAM • SHEILA INGRAM • TANIA INGRAM • CHLOE ISGROVE • TRACEY ISGROVE • MISS C LOUISE ISLIP • MISS SIAN M ISLIP • MR & MRS S R ISLIP • JACK & MORGAN • PETER JACKSON • ANDREW JAMES • ANDREW JAMES • ANDY JAMES • ANDY JAMES • ANTHONY JAMES • BARRIE JAMES • DANIEL JAMES • DAVID JAMES • ELLA-SIONED JAMES • GARETH JAMES • GAYNOR JAMES • GWYNNE FRANKLIN JAMES • HARVEY JAMES • HUW FRANKLIN JAMES • JACK JAMES • JOAN & AMY JAMES • KAYE JAMES • KEVIN JAMES • MISS TRACY JAMES • MOYRA JAMES • MR ANDREW JAMES • MR COLIN JAMES • MRS ALISON JAMES • NIC JAMES • REBECCA JAMES • ROBERT LEIGH JAMES • SARAH JAMES • TERRY JAMES • SANDRA JAMES JEFFERIES • BARBARA JAMES LLOYD • PHILIP JAN BAACA • CHRIS JEFFERIES • ANDREW JENKINS • D JOHN JENKINS • DENNIS JENKINS • DOUGLAS JENKINS • GARETH JENKINS • GARETH JENKINS • HANNAH JENKINS • IEUAN RHYS JENKINS • ISAAC JENKINS • JOHN JENKINS • KEITH JENKINS • LEWIS JENKINS • LUCY JENKINS • MICHELE JENKINS •NEIL JENKINS • NEIL JENKINS • NOAH JENKINS • RACHEL JENKINS • RACHEL JENKINS • RHYS JENKINS • RHYS JENKINS • RHYS JENKINS • RICHARD JENKINS • ROBERT JENKINS • RYAN CARWYN JENKINS • SHEILA JENKINS • SOPHIE JENKINS • SUSAN JENKINS • TERRY JENKINS • TIM JENKINS • YUMIKO JENKINS • HUGH DAVID JENKINS • JOHN HUGH JENKINS • SIAN LOUISE JENKINS • SIAN LOUISE JENKINS • KEITH JENNINGS • ANTHONY JOHJANSEN • JUSTIN JOHN JOHN • NIGEL G JOHN • OSMONDE G JOHN OBE • HELEN JOHNS • KEVIN JOHNS • OWEN JOHNS • SCOTT JOHNS • ADRIAN JOHNSON • BARBARA JANE JOHNSON • BEVERLEY JOHNSON • CHRIS JOHNSON • CHRIS JOHNSON • CRAIG JOHNSON • CRAIG JOHNSON • CRAIG JOHNSON • DAVID JOHNSON • DEBBIE JOHNSON • JANE JOHNSON • RACHEL JOHNSON • RACHEL JOHNSON • RACHEL JOHNSON • STEPHEN ROBERT JOHNSON • ANDREW JOLLIFFE • MALCOLM JOLLIFFE • ABIGAIL JONES • ADRIAN JONES • ALED JONES • ALED JONES • ALFYN JONES • ALISON JANE JONES • ALLEN JONES • ALUN LEWIS JONES • AMANDA JONES • AMANDA JONES • ANDREA JONES • ANDREA JONES • ANDREW JONES • ANDREW JONES •ANEURYN JONES • ANGHARAD JONES • ANITA JONES • ANN E JONES • ANNETTE JONES • ANNETTE JONES • ANTHONY JONES • BEATRICE JONES • BENNETT JONES • BLEDDYN R JONES • BROGAN JONES • BRYN GRANVILLE HUGHES JONES • BRYNMOR WILLIAM JONES • CALLUM M M JONES • CAMERON JONES • CAROL JONES • CAROLINE JONES • CARWYN JONES • CHRISTINE JONES • CLIVE JONES • CLIVE DEREK JONES • D MICHAEL M JONES • DAN JONES • DANIEL JONES • DANIEL JONES • DARREN MARC JONES • DARREN MARC JONES • DARREN R JONES • DAVE 'OXO' JONES • DAVID JONES • DAVID JONES • DAVID H JONES • DAVID R JONES • DAVID RHYS JONES • DAVID STEPHEN JONES

THE FANS J-L

DAVID WYN JONES • DEBBIE JONES • DEBRA JONES • DEIAN JONES • DELWYN EWEN JONES • DOGGY JONES • DUNCAN JONES • DYLAN PAUL WYN JONES • EDWARD JONES • EDWARD GLYN JONES • ELEN JONES • ELIS LLOYD JONES • ELIZABETH JONES • EMMA JONES • EMMA JONES • EMMA LAUREN JONES • GARETH JOHN JONES • GARETH THOMAS JONES • GARY JONES • GARY J JONES • GAYNOR JONES • GERAINT JONES • GETHIN JONES • GETHIN JONES • GLYN DAVID JONES • GRAHAM JONES • GRAHAM JONES • GWYN JONES •GWYNETH JONES • HANNAH JONES • HAYDN JONES • HEATHER FIONA JONES • HELEN JONES • HYWEL 'H' JONES • IESTYN JONES • IEUAN JONES • ISOBEL JONES • ISOBEL JONES • IWAN JONES • IWAN JONES • IWAN ELIS JONES • JANE E JONES • JEAN JONES • JEMMA JONES • JENNA JONES • JOHN DAVID JONES • JOY V JONES • KATIE JONES • KAYLIE JONES • LIONEL B JONES • LIZ JONES • LIZ JONES • LORRIE JONES • LOUISE JONES • LOUISE JONES • LUKE ROBERT DAVID JONES • LYNNE JONES • LYNNETTE JONES • MARI JONES • MARILYN WYN JONES • MARTYN JONES • MARTYN JONES • MARTYN JONES • MAT JONES • MATTHEW JONES • MAUREEN JONES • MELODY JONES • MERVYN JONES • MIA SIAN JONES • MICHAEL JONES • MICHAEL C H JONES • MORGAN JONES • MORLAIS JONES • NIA LAUREN JONES • NICK JONES • OLIVER JONES • PAMELA CHRISTINE JONES • PAUL JONES • PAUL JONES • PAUL JONES • PAULA JONES • PETER JONES • PETER THOMAS JONES • PHILIP JONES • PHILIP JONES • PHILIP ADAM JONES • PHILLIP JONES • RAYMOND JONES • REBECCA SIAN JONES • REBECKA LUCY JONES • RHIA JONES • RHIANNON T JONES • RHODRI JONES • RHODRI JONES • RHODRI JONES • RICHARD JONES • RICHARD F W C JONES • ROB JONES • ROBERT JONES • ROBERT JONES • ROBERT IAN JONES • ROGER JONES • RYAN RHYS JONES • SABRINA JONES • SADIE JONES • SALLY JONES • SARAH JONES • SARAH JONES • SARAH JONES • SARAH HOWARD JONES • STEPHEN JONES • STEPHEN GARETH JONES • SUSAN ANN JONES • SUZY JONES • TAFF JONES • TERRY JONES • THERESA JONES • THOMAS HENRY JONES • THOMAS JEFFREY CECIL JONES • THOMAS PATRICK JONES • TIM JONES •TIMOTHY JONES • TIMOTHY G JONES • TOM JONES • TONY JONES • TRACEY CHRISTINE JONES • TREFOR GLYN JONES • TREFOR RHYS JONES • TREVOR BANBURY JONES • TUDOR JONES • VIV & ANNE JONES • VIVIAN JONES• WAYNE JONES • WILLIAM JONES • WILLIAM JONES • YOAN JONES • ALWYN H JONES • RICHARD & MARGARET JONES • MIKE JONES MRCVS • MIKE JONES MRCVS • JAN JONES-DAVIES • NEIL JONES-DAVIES • GWENJONES-EDWARDS • HELEN JONES-VANS • CHRISTOPHER MICHAEL JORDAN • JAMES MICHAEL JORDAN • JODIE JORDAN • JUNE MARY BRIDGET JORDAN • LISA MARIE JORDAN • RICHARD CHRISTOPHER JORDAN • OWAINJOYNSON • ADRIAN THOMASJUDD • HANNAH JUDD • LIBBY JUDD • TOMOS JUDD • KED • DAVE KEEFE • GEORGE KEEFE • HENRY KEEFE • PAT KEEFE • CHLOE KEENE • CHLOE KEENE • CHLOE KEENE • ANTHONY KELLY • RACHEL KELLY • REBECCA KELLY • JOANNE KENNEY • MORGAN KENNEY • RHIANNON KENNEY • TREVOR KENNEY • LUCY-ROSE KENT • NICKY KENT • OWEN KENT • CHARLIE KENYON • RUTH KENYON •STEVE KENYON • DEBBIE KERR • GARETH KERR • IAN KERR • DAVID A KILLA • SEREN KILLPARTRICK • LEAH KINCHIN • RHYS DAVID KING • ROBERT PAUL KING • RYAN DEREK KING • DANIEL KINGSCOTT-EDMUNDS • JAMIE KINGSCOTT-EDMUNDS • MAUREEN KIRBY • SHAWN KIRK • JESSE DYLAN KIRKHAM • ANDREW KITSCHKER • MARILYN KNIGHT • RICHARD KNIGHT • PAUL KUBIT • PAUL KUBIT • PAUL KUBIT • DANIEL LACEY • ALYSSIA LAKE • BECKY LAKEY • SIAN LAKEY • PHILIP LAMBE • PHILIP LAMBE • DAVID LAMBETH • PETER LANE • CHRISTOPHER LANG • DAVID LANG • MERRILL LANG • NICOLA LANG • BETHANY LANGFORD • CORENE LANGFORD • OSCAR LANGFORD • BRYONY MAIR LANGMAID • EMMA LOUISE LANGMAID • JONATHAN CHARLES JAMES LANGMAID • TIMOTHY PAUL LANGMAID • BRIONILANGSDALE • CARYS LANGSDALE • JACK LANGSDALE • OLIVER LANGSDALE • LARGE • BARRIE LASKEY • IZAAK IOSEF LASKEY • KRISTIAN LASKEY • ZEBASTIEN HUNTER LASKEY • PHILIP LASSETER • SIMON LASSETER • KELLY LATIMER • MAISIE LATIMER • CARLA LAVARACK • GARETH LAWLESS • MIKE LAWLESS • DAVID C LAWRENCE • DAVID C LAWRENCE • DAVID G LAWRENCE • MARK LAWRENCE • PAUL LAWRENCE • LLEWELLYN LAYTON • LLEWELLYN LAYTON • LLEWELLYN LAYTON • AARON LEA • DAVID LEA • DONNA LEA • STEFFAN LEA • EMMA LOUISE LEABACK • GRIFF LEADER • VICKY LEECH • STEVEN JAMES DAVID LEIGH • WILLIAM JAMES PETER LEIGH • ISABELLA LEMPRIERE • ALICE LENTON • GAYNOR MADOCLEONARD • JOHN LEONARD • LEONARD • ADRIAN LEWIS • ALED LEWIS • ALEX LEWIS • ANDREA LEWIS • ANDY LEWIS • ANDY LEWIS • ANDY LEWIS • ANTHONY LEWIS • BETHAN LEWIS • BETHAN LEWIS • CALLUM RYLAND LEWIS • DAVID NICHOLAS LEWIS • EDWARD LEWIS • EUAN RICHARD LEWIS • GARETH DAVID LEWIS • GLYNDWR LEWIS • GWYN LEWIS• HANNA JEAN LEWIS • HUW JAMES LEWIS • IRIS LEWIS • ISABEL KATHLEEN LEWIS • JAC LEWIS • JAMES LEWIS • JAMES LEWIS • JAMIE LEWIS •JAYNELOUISE LEWIS • JEFFREY LEWIS • JEREMY RYLAND LEWIS • JON LEWIS • JON LEONARD LEWIS • JORDAN LEWIS • KEITH LEWIS • KERI ANN LEWIS • KEVIN LEWIS • KIRSTEN LEWIS • KIRSTEN LEWIS • LYN LEWIS • MARTYN LEWIS • MATTHEW LEWIS • MATTHEW JAMES LEWIS • MAUREEN LEWIS • MICHAEL JAMES OLIVER LEWIS • MILLIE LEWIS • MITCHELL LEWIS • NICKI LEWIS •NYELEWIS • OLIVER JOHN LEWIS • OWEN LEWIS • PAUL LEWIS • RACHAEL LOUISE LEWIS • RALPH LEWIS • RHYDIAN LEWIS • RHYS LEWIS • RYAN LLOYD LEWIS • TERRY LEWIS • TRACY LEWIS • BRYAN LEWIS JONES • ISLWYN LEWIS JONES • RUTH LEWIS JONES • DAVID NICHOLAS LEWIS JUNIOR (RIP) • ERICA LEYSHON • GARETH LEYSHON • CATHY LIGHT • CATHY LIGHT • HELEN LIGHT • JOHN LIGHT • NATHAN LIGHT • PAUL LIGHT • PAUL LIGHT • MARY LIGHT PATEL • ALFIE EMLYN LIGHTFOOT • AMELIA MAY LIGHTFOOT • CHRISTOPHER ANDREW LIGHTFOOT • HARRY VAUGHAN LIGHTFOOT • ANNA LINDGREN • ANNE LITTLEJOHNS • PETER LITTLEJOHNS • CORRIN LIVINGSTONE • GRANT LIVINGSTONE • HUGH LIVINGSTONE • TREVOR LIVINGSTONE • MARK LLEWELLYN •

THE FANS L-N

ROBERT LLEWELLYN • BARRY LLEWELYN • PAUL LLEWELYN • THOMAS PAUL LLEWELYN • AMY LLOYD • CARWYN LLOYD • DAFYDD OWEN LLOYD • DAVID LLOYD • DES LLOYD • EMMA LLOYD • GARETH IDWAL LLOYD • IOAN LLOYD • JANET LLOYD • JOAN LLOYD • JOHN LLOYD • KEV LLOYD • MARTIN DAVID LLOYD • MATTHEW LLOYD • PAMELA LLOYD • RALPH LLOYD • RICKY LLOYD • SARAH LLOYD • SUSAN LLOYD • TAMZIN GRACE LLOYD • TRACEY LLOYD • TULLULAH GRACE LLOYD • DANIEL JAMES LLOYD-THOMAS • EMMA LLOYD-TRAVERS • LLYFF • STEVE LOCK • ELUN LOCKE • PAUL LOCKE • SAMUEL LOCKE • JACK LONG • MORGAN LONG • NICOLA LONG • RICHARD LONG • DONNA LONGHURST • KEVIN LONGHURST • LOWRI LONGHURST • LEUAN LOPEZ • DANIELLE LORION • ADRIAN LOTE • CALUM LOTE • DEBBY LOTE • STAN LOTE • STEVEN LUCAS • CYNTHIA LUNT • PHILIP LUNT • BARBARA LYDDON • JOHN LYDDON • ANNE LYNCH • TONY LYNCH • IFOR LYNWEN • ABIGAIL MACFARLANE • ABIGAIL MACFARLANE • FINLEY MACFARLANE • FINLEY MACFARLANE • STUART MACFARLANE • STUART MACFARLANE • TRACEY MACGILLIVRAY • MARGARET MACINNES • PHILIP MACKIE • NIGEL MADDOCK • RACHEL MADELEY • RICHARD JOHN MAGNESS • ANN MAHER • IAN MAHER • KEVIN MAHONEY • KEVIN MAHONEY • DEBORAH MAIDMENT • LEWIS MAIDMENT • PAUL MAIDMENT • RICCARDO MANCINO • PAUL MANSON • PAUL MANSON • PAUL MANSON • RUPERT MARCHINGTON • ALLAN MARGERISON • ALLAN MARGERISON • MARI • CHRIS MARKWELL • DIANE MARKWELL • GLYN MARKWELL • SARA MARSH • THOMAS MARSH • GREGOR MARSLAND • ROSIE MARTIN • AMY MASON • ANDREW MASON • BEN MASON • CHRIS MASON • CLIVE MASON • DAVID MASON • ERIC SAMUEL JAMES MASON • FFION MASON • GARETH MASON • HELEN MASON • HOWARD MASON • TASHA MASON • VICKY MASON • EMMA MASSINGHAM • CAROL MATTHEWS • DAVID MATTHEWS • JOSHUA JAMES MATTHEWS • JOYCE MATTHEWS • LUKE JOHN MATTHEWS • SARAH MATTHEWS • JILL MAXTED • STEPHEN MAXTED • HELEN MAXWELL • ISLA MAXWELL • DAVID MAY • GWENLLIAN MCATEER • GWYNETH MCATEER • PATRICK MCATEER • DAVID MCBRIDE • SHERREN MCCABE-FINLAYSON •SAM MCCAFFERTY • EWAN TOMOS KEITH MCCALLUM • EWAN TOMOS KEITH MCCALLUM • EWAN TOMOS KEITH MCCALLUM • EWAN TOMOS KEITH MCCALLUM • FREYA SEREN MCCALLUM • FREYASEREN MCCALLUM • FREYA SEREN MCCALLUM • FREYA SEREN MCCALLUM • SOPHIE MCCLUGGAGE • OSIAN MCCOY • MCDERMOTT • SUSAN MCGUIRE • ROBERT MCKINNON • JANE MCKINNON-JOHNSON • SCOTT MCMILLAN •SOPHIE MCMILLAN • EVAN & GRACE MCNAMEE • EVAN & GRACE MCNAMEE • EVAN & GRACE MCNAMEE • KEV MCNAMEE• KEV MCNAMEE • KEV MCNAMEE • BABY BOY MEADOWCROFT • BABY BOY MEADOWCROFT • JEREMY MEADOWCROFT • JEREMY MEADOWCROFT • DORIAN MEDLICOTT • HAYLEY MEDLICOTT • LEIGH MEDLICOTT • MEGAN • HUW MEREDITH • JOHN MEREDITH • RHYS MEREDITH • SALLY MEREDITH • ELERI MESSHAM • MICHAEL • MICHELLE • LIZ MILES • MANDY MILLERS • HUW MILTON • MILLIE MILTON • PAULA MILTON • REBECCA MILTON • TERRY MILTON • JEFF MINCHER • BETHAN MITCHELL •COLIN G MITCHELL • COLIN G MITCHELL • DAMIAN MITCHELL • RACHEL EMMA MITCHELL • CATHY MITCHELMORE • CATHY MITCHELMORE • CLAIRE MITCHELMORE • CLAIRE MITCHELMORE • DYLAN MITCHELMORE • DYLAN MITCHELMORE • IAN MITCHELMORE • IAN MITCHELMORE • JAMES OWAIN MITHAN • MATTHEW RHYS MITHAN • MO • MONTY • BOB MOONEY • SYLVIA MOONEY • ABBIE MOORE • AMY MOORE • CATH MOORE • JEN MOORE • KATHERINE MOORE • NATALIE MOORE • NATALIE MOORE • NEIL MOORE • RICHARD MOORE • SUSAN MOORE • TRICIA MOORE • CHARLOTTE FRANCESCA MOORE • CHARLOTTE FRANCESCA MOORE • JACOB THOMAS MOORE • JACOB THOMAS MOORE • NICHOLAS JAMES MOORE • NICHOLAS JAMES MOORE • OLIVIA GRACE MOORE • OLIVIA GRACE MOORE • ADEN GLYN MORGAN • ANDREW D MORGAN • ANDREW G MORGAN • CHARLES MORGAN • CHRISTINE L MORGAN • CHRISTOPHER MORGAN • DAVID MORGAN • DAVID J MORGAN•DAVID W MORGAN • GAVIN MORGAN • GUZZA MORGAN • HUW GLYN MORGAN • KATHERINE MORGAN • KERI MORGAN • LYNDON J G MORGAN • LYNNE MORGAN • NELSON MORGAN • PAMELA MORGAN • RHYS MORGAN • STEPHANIE V MORGAN • STEVEN JOHN MORGAN • STUART MORGAN • IEUAN MORLAIS MORGAN • ANDREW D MORGAN JONES• GWEN MORGAN JONES • HELEN MORGAN JONES • MARI MORGAN JONES • SIAN MORGAN • CALLUM MORGANS • CEIRAN MORGANS • LEE MORGANS • AMANDA MORLE • LAURA MORLE • NICKY MORLE • PHIL MORLE • BRYAN MORLEY • CAROL MORLEY • AMANDA MORRIS • AMY MORRIS • ANDREW MORRIS • ANDREW MORRIS • BETHAN MORRIS • CAROL MORRIS • DANIEL MORRIS • DANIEL N R MORRIS • DAVID MORRIS • DEBORAH MORRIS • ELINOR MORRIS • EMILY MORRIS • EMMA MORRIS • GARETH MORRIS • GARYTH HUW MORRIS • HELEN MORRIS • JAMES P R MORRIS • JANET MORRIS • JOHN MORRIS • JONNY MORRIS • KATE MORRIS • KATE MORRIS • KEVIN R MORRIS • MARSHALL MORRIS • NICOLA MORRIS • RHIANNON MORRIS • RHYS MORRIS • SARA MORRIS• SHAUNA C MORRIS • SIAN MORRIS • STEVE MORRIS • VERONICA MORRIS • WAYNE MORRIS • BARBARA MORRIS-BROWN • IEUAN MORRIS-BROWN • OLIVIA MORRIS-ROWN • EDWARD G A MORSE • GARETH E MORSE • SKYE MORSE • WENDY P MORSE • ANTHONY MOSELEY • ANTHONY MOSELEY • ELAINE MOSELEY • FIONA MOSELEY • FIONA MOSELEY • GWYN MOSELEY • TERENCE MOSELEY • ANTHONY DAVID MOUNT • STEVE MULLEN • MARIA MULVIHILL • KAREN MURPHY RYE • CRAIG MURTAGH • THOMAS MUSAHL • KATE MYNOTT • JACK NAGLE • NIC NAISH • ANDREA NAPIER • GREGOR NAPIER • ENYA NARBETT • IESTYN NARBETT • KEVIN NARBETT • PHOEBE NARBETT • JANET NASH • JOSHUA NASH • NORMAN NASH • ZEB NASH • MORGANE NAVARRO • TINA NEAL • DAWN NEEDHAM • MACSEN NEEDHAM • MARK NEEDHAM • PAUL NEEDHAM • SION NEEDHAM • TOMMY NEEDHAM • TRACEY NEEDHAM • MICHAEL NELSON • RAY NELSON • MICHAEL NENER • NERYS • CRAIG NEWBERY-JONES • LES NEWELL • FRAYA NEWHAM • PAUL NEWTON • SUZANNE NEWTON • NIA • KIM NICHOL • NICHOLAS • CATHARINA NICHOLLS •

THE FANS N-P

DEAN NICHOLLS • HAYLEY NICHOLLS • HOWARD NICHOLLS • KEVIN & BARRY NICHOLLS • LUCY NICHOLLS • LUCY NICHOLLS • MARK NICHOLLS • PAUL NICHOLLS • MOLLIE MARIE NIGHTINGALE • NINA • JOHN NORMAN (THE WEATHERMAN) • MRS CHRISTINE NORTON • KERRY NOTTAGE • CEINWEN NUGENT • FFION NUGENT • JAMES NUGENT • JUAN LUIS NUTE • JAMES MICHAEL OATES • BETHAN O'BRIEN • BETHAN O'BRIEN • LIZ O'BRIEN • LIZ O'BRIEN • TERENCE PATRICK O'HARA • BEV O'LEARY • GEOFF O'LEARY • MATHEW O'LEARY • SIMON O'LEARY • CAROL OLIVER • NICK OLIVER • HAYLEY A O'SHEA • NICOLAS OST • SIAN OST • MIKE O'SULLIVAN • SUSAN OVERTON • OWAIN • ANTHONY JOHN OWEN • ARWEL LLECHID A DAWN OWEN • DANIEL OWEN • DAYTON OWEN • ELLIW MALI OWEN • JAMIE OWEN • JOY OWEN • KARL OWEN • KARL OWEN • KARL OWEN • KIERA OWEN • MARK OWEN • MORGAN ELLIS OWEN • PHILIP OWEN • SHARON OWEN • STEPHEN OWEN • OWEN • DANIEL OWEN-RIJNENBERG • IIESHA OWEN-RIJNENBERG • MIA OWEN-RIJNENBERG • EDWINA OWENS • EDWINA OWENS • GRAHAM BARRIE OWENS • GRAHAM BARRIE OWENS • MORRIS R OWENS • SHEILA M OWENS • DAVID PACKER • SHARON PACKER • TEGAN PACKER • KEITH NOEL PADFIELD • KEITH NOEL PADFIELD • KEITH NOEL PADFIELD • KEITH NOEL PADFIELD • EDWINPAGE • KEITH PAGE • LIAM PAGE • MALCOM PAGE • CHRIS PAGLIONICO • KIRSTY PALFREY • DEBBIE PALMER • FRAN PALMER • LIAM PALMER • LUCY PALMER • SAM PALMER • FERNANDO CORREA PANDO • ANDREW PARKER • JENNIFER PARKER • JOHN PARKER • KATIE PARKER • STEPHEN PARKER • BURNETTE PARKMAN • JOHN PARKMAN • ALFIE PARRY • DR MARTIN GRATTON PARRY • HUGH R PARRY • JENNIFER ANN PARRY • JOHN (PAFF) PARRY • JOHN (PAFF)PARRY • JULIA PARRY • KENNETH GORDON PARRY • NELL PARRY • STEPHEN JOHN PARRY • VICTOR PARRY • VICTORIA PARRY • HANNAH PARSONS • HARRY JAMES PARSONS • JOHN SELLICK PARSONS • IAN MICHAEL PARSONS • DR NIKIN PATEL • HAIDEN PATEL • NEIL PATEL • BEVERLEY PATTERSON-JONES • DEIAN PATTERSON-JONES • KEVIN PATTERSON-JONES • ASUTOSH PAUL • PAUL • EIDDON GWYN ASUTOSH PAUL • EIFION JOHN MAELON PAUL • MARY ELIZABETH PAUL • JON PAYNE • SAM PAYNE • ALEXANDER PEACHEY • JAMES PEACHEY • LINDA PEACOCK • LINDA PEACOCK • COLIN DAVID PEARCE • STEPHEN J PEGUM • JUAN PEREZ • ALUN PERKINS • DAVID PERKINS • GARETH PERKINS • MANDY PERKINS • BERNADETTE PERRETT • GERRARD PERRETT • PHILLIP PERRETT • STANLEY PERRETT • MARTYN PERRIN • SIAN PERRIN • DAVID PERRY • ALUN PERVIN • MARTYN PERVIN • ELIZABETH JOAN PETERS • KENNETH PETERS • MARK PETERS • AMY PHILLIPS • ANDREW PHILLIPS • ARTHUR PHILLIPS • BERWYN PHILLIPS • BLEDDYN PHILLIPS • CARLEY PHILLIPS • DAFYDD PHILLIPS • DYLAN PHILLIPS • DYLAN PHILLIPS • DYLAN PHILLIPS • ELAINE PHILLIPS • ELLIOT PHILLIPS • EMILY PHILLIPS • GARETH PHILLIPS • GEORGI PHILLIPS • HARRY PHILLIPS • HARRY PHILLIPS • HARRY PHILLIPS • HENRY PHILLIPS • JACOB PHILLIPS • JAMES PHILLIPS • JAMES PHILLIPS • JAMES PHILLIPS • JAMES PHILLIPS • JOSHUA PHILLIPS • MANDY PHILLIPS • MATT PHILLIPS • MAX PHILLIPS • MAX PHILLIPS • MAX PHILLIPS • NIGEL PHILLIPS • TOM PHILLIPS • ANDY PHILPIN • LOLA PHILPIN • RHYS PHILPIN • SHARON PHILPIN • ANDREA R PICKERING • CLAIRE PICKERING • ALEX PICOUTO • ALEXANDER DAVID PICOUTO • ANNA KATRINA PIECHOTA • ANNA KATRINA PIECHOTA • HELEN PLATT • STEVE PLATT • JONATHAN PLEAVIN • SARAH PLEAVIN • SUSIE PLUNKETT • CHÉ POMPHREY • BEVERLEY POOLE • DEREK R POOLE • JENNIFER G POOLE • KEN POOLE • STEPHEN J G POOLE • MARIA DE LOS ANGELES PORRAS-CHAPMAN • GUY JAMES RICHARD POULTER • RICHARD POULTER • ADAM POWELL • ALAN POWELL • AMBER POWELL • DANIEL POWELL • DARREN POWELL • DARREN POWELL • DELME POWELL • DENNIS POWELL • DONNA POWELL • HANNAH POWELL • HUW POWELL • IAN POWELL • LUCY POWELL • VERNON POWELL • JON PRATT • ALLAN PRICE • DAVID PRICE • DENNIS PRICE • ELEN PRICE • GARETH PRICE • GETHIN PRICE • IAN PRICE • IVY PRICE • JOSHUA TOMOS PRICE • JOSHUA TOMOS PRICE • KEVIN PRICE •

THE FANS P-S

LUKE PRICE • MATTHEW PRICE • MOLLY PRICE • MORGAN ASHDOWN PRICE • NIA PRICE • RICHARD PRICE • TOBY LLEWELYN PRICE • TOBY LLEWELYN PRICE • TOMAS PRICE • TRACEY PRICE • ALISON PRICE-JONES • CLWYD PRICE-JONES • ANTHONY PRINCE • IESTYN PRINCE • ANNA PRIOR • JAN & JON PRIOR • JENNI PRIOR • SHAN PRIOR • ALED PRITCHARD • ALED PRITCHARD • STEPHEN PRITCHARD • SUE PRITCHARD • ARCHIE PROBERT • CHLOE PROBERT • DAMIAN HARVEY PROBERT • DAVID ALLAN PROBERT • DYLAN PROBERT • EVAN DAVID PROBERT • KEN PROBERT • MARJORIE PROBERT • MORGAN RHYS PROBERT • GLYNNE PROSSER • LYN PROSSER • RHYDIAN PROSSER • SARA PROSSER • TOMOS PROSSER • A PROUD • MATHEW PRYCE • RHIANNON PRYCE-WILLIS • JESSIE PUGH • KERENA PUGH • LEWIS PUGH • STEPHEN PUGH • JULIAN PURCHASE • NICHOLAS PURNELL • ROBERT PURNELL • TRACY PURNELL • VICKY PURNELL • EUAN PURVIS • THOMAS PURVIS • DYLAN JOHN PYKE • LYNDSAY RAE • BETHAN RALPH • JAMES RALPH • MARK RALPH • MELANIE RALPH • BETHAN RAMSAY • HANNAH RAMSAY • OWEN RAMSAY • STEPHEN RAMSAY • PHILLIP RANDALL • ABBIE RANDS • DAISY RANDS • DEAN RANDS • KATIE RANDS • CHRISTINA REARDON • SIMON REECE • MARK ANDREW REED • AMBER REES • ANNI REES • BENJAMIN 'BEANS' REES • BETHAN 'BARRY' REES • CASEY REES • CYRIL REES • DAVE REES • DAVID REES • DAVID REES • DAWN REES • DOUGLAS 'TAFFY' REES • DOUGLAS 'TAFFY' REES • DYLAN T REES • EVAN T REES • GARETH J REES • GERWYN REES • GRAHAM REES • GREG D REES • JAMES THE BOY REES • JANET REES • JASON REES • JOSH REES • KAREN REES • KAREN REES • MARC REES • MARTIN K REES • MARTIN K REES • MERVYN REES • SAMUEL REES • SARAH REES • SHERIDAN REES • STEPHEN REES • T NELVILLE REES • TEGAN M REES • TIM B REES • BRYONY REES-WINTER • JAMIE REES-WINTER • JAMIE REES-WINTER • VICKI REES-WINTER • ALAN REYNOLDS • DAVID REYNOLDS • NYLE REYNOLDS • VICTORIA REYNOLDS • VICTORIA REYNOLDS • RHODRI • RHYS • BEN RICHARDS • CATRIN RICHARDS • CHARLIE RICHARDS • DIANA RICHARDS • JASON RICHARDS • JOHN RICHARDS • MARK DAVID RICHARDS • OWEN RICHARDS • RACHEL RICHARDS • RAY RICHARDS • RHODRI RICHARDS • SIAN RICHARDS • TIM RICHARDS • WILLIAM RICHARDS • ZOE ALEXIS RICHARDS • CAITLIN RICHARDS-JONES • CAITLIN RICHARDS-JONES • JOHN RICHARDS-JONES • JOHN RICHARDS-JONES • NICK RICHARDS-JONES • NICKRICHARDS-JONES • DAVID IVOR RIDGWAY • OWAIN DAVID RIDGWAY • SEREN JANE RIDGWAY • TRACEY JANE RIDGWAY • DAVID RIFFEL • SANDY RIFFEL • ALEX RIGGS • IAN RIGGS • JACK RIGGS • JASON RIGGS • KATHERINE RIGGS • MEG RIGGS • THOMAS RIGGS • RILLA • AARON ROBERTS • ALED HELIN ROBERTS ROBERTS • ASHLEY ROBERTS • BRYN ROBERTS • CHRISTOPHER ROBERTS • CYNAN LLOYD ROBERTS • GARETH ROBERTS • GERAINT ROBERTS • HELEN ROBERTS • HEULWEN (SUNNY) ROBERTS • HEULWEN (SUNNY) ROBERTS • JAC ROBERTS • JACK ROBERTS • JOHN ROBERTS • KAREN ROBERTS • LLEW ROBERTS • LLEWLYN OWEN ROBERTS • LLOYD ROBERTS • LORRAINE ROBERTS • MATT ROBERTS • PAUL ROBERTS • PHIL ROBERTS • RACHEL ROBERTS • RACHEL ANNE ROBERTS • SIAN ROBERTS • VINCE ROBERTS • VINCE ROBERTS • WILLIAM NEIL ROBERTS • DAFYDD ROBERTS-HARRY • JANICE ROBINSON • JANICE ROBINSON • JASON DENIS ROBINSON • JASON DENIS ROBINSON • PAUL ROBINSON • RAYMOND ROBINSON • KIERAN ROD • STEVE ROD • TINA ROD • ANGHARAD RODERICK • IESTYN RODERICK • SELWYN RODERICK • ALEX ROGERS • ALISA ROGERS • BRYAN ROGERS • GEORGINA ROGERS • IAN ROGERS • JEFF ROGERS • MAUREEN ROGERS • PETE ROGERS • PETE ROGERS • PIP ROGERS • SAM ROGERS • JAC MICHAEL ROSCOE • AMY ROWLANDS • ANDREW ROWLANDS • BENJAMIN ROWLANDS • DANIEL ROWLANDS • MATTHEW ROWLANDS • ANTHONY ROWLES • OLIVIA J ROWLES • SUMMER J ROWLES • STEPHANIE ROWLEY • CHARLOTTE ELIZABETH ROWSE • JAMES GRENVILLE ROWSE • KAYLEIGH ROYLE • KAYLEIGH ROYLE • KAYLEIGH ROYLE • GARTH RUNDLE • PETER RUSHMORE • AMY RYAN • EMILY RYAN • JEFF RYAN • KATRENA RYAN • CATHERINE RYDER • DEREK RYDER • OLI RYDER • ALAN SAINSBURY • MITCHELL SALES •

THE FANS S-T

DORON SALOMON • TREVOR SALOMON • LEIDA SALWAY • EDWARD SAMWAYS • JACOB O SANDERS • TOM J SANDERS • BRYN SAYCE • CARRIE SAYCE • RHIANNON SAYCE • TANYA-MARIE SAYCE • ADAM SAYE • CHARLOTTE SAYE • DENISE SAYE • PAUL SAYE • LES SCARBOROUGH • PHYLL SCARBOROUGH • MARK SCHROEDER • MARK SCOTT • JAMES H SCOURFIELD • SCRUM • CINDY SEBOEK • MAY LING SEHO - EVANS • TOM SELDON • SONAL SHAH • SIAN SHÂW • LYN SHEARS • TREVOR SHEARS • MARTYN SHEEHAN • MARTYN SHEEHAN • DYLAN SHELLEY • JESSICA SHEPHERD • MARK SHEPHERD • MICHAEL SHEPHERD • ABBY SHEPPARD • MARK SHEPPARD • RACHEL SHEPPARD • ATSUHIDE SHIOJIRI • SORA SHIOJIRI • AEDDAN SHIPP • GARIN SHIPP • OSIAN SHIPP • RICHARD SHIPP • NORTON SHORT • ETHAN SIEVEWRIGHT • HENRY SIEVEWRIGHT • KENNETH CHRISTOPHER SIEVEWRIGHT • TOBIAS SIEVEWRIGHT • CRAIG SIMOX • FFION SIMOX • MABLI SIMOX • MATI SIMOX • NEIL SIMS • MARK WILLIAM SINFIELD • DAVID JOHN SINGLETON • SIWAN • CHRIS SLOCOMBE • CHRIS SLOCOMBE • DANIEL SLOCOMBE • DANIEL SLOCOMBE • MICHAEL SLOCOMBE • SANDRA SLOCOMBE • SANDRA SLOCOMBE • SMALL • ANDREA SMITH • ANDY SMITH • BARRY SMITH • BEN SMITH • CARYS MAY SMITH • CHARLENE SMITH • CHERYL SMITH • CRAIG SMITH • CRAIG SMITH • DAVID SMITH • DAVID SMITH • DAVID SMITH • ELLIE LOUISE SMITH • GERALLT OWAIN SMITH • GLYNDWR SMITH • HUW SMITH • JAMIE BRYAN SMITH • JEREMY SMITH • KATHERINE SMITH • KIRSTY SMITH • LAURA D SMITH • LESLEY A SMITH • LOUISE SMITH • MARJORIE RICHMAL SMITH • MIKE 'FOZZIE' SMITH • MIKE 'FOZZIE' SMITH • MORGAN BRYAN SMITH • MR NEIL J SMITH • NIGEL SMITH • PHIL RABY SMITH • REBECCA SMITH • REBECCA SMITH • REBECCCA SMITH • RHYS WILLIAM SMITH • ROBIN SMITH • RUBYSMITH • SANDRA SMITH • SHIRLEY MARGRETTA SMITH • SPENCER GAVIN SMITH • STEVE SMITH • STUART MICHAEL SMITH • SUE SMITH • TERESA SMITH • VICTORIA SMITH • WILLIAM JOSEPH SMITH • DELYTH SPEAKMAN • DEWI SPEAKMAN • EMILY SPEAKMAN • MEGAN SPEAKMAN • ANGHARAD SPECK • KEITH SPECK • LYNN SPECK • RHIANNON SPECK • SIAN SPECK • STEPHANIE ANNE SPELLER • STEPHANIE ANNE FRANCIS SPELLER • ALICE SPENCER • RYAN SPENCER • MIKE SPIERS • KATHRYN SPIERS-PRITCHARD • MEGAN SPIERS-PRITCHARD • TOM SPILLANE • MEGAN SQUIRE • PETER SQUIRE • BETHAN STACEY • DEREK STACEY • JAYNE STACEY • ZOE LOUISE STAFFORD • ZOE LOUISE STAFFORD • ZOE LOUISE STAFFORD • ZOE LOUISE STAFFORD • JACK DYLAN STAINSBY • JACK DYLAN STAINSBY • JIMMY THOMAS STAINSBY • JIMMY THOMAS STAINSBY • GARIN STANDING • CONSTANCE STEPHENS • MARTYN STEPHENS • ROY STEPHENS • GAIL STEPHENSON • HEDLEY STEPHENSON • DARREN STERRY • JACKIE STEVENS • PETER STEVENS • OWEN STICKINGS • RAYMOND STIFF • ANTHONY STINGL • CLAIRE STINGL • MATTHEW STINGL • RICHARD STINGL • JASON L STOKES • KEITH STONE • ALAN STRANGE • AMANDA STRANGE • CERYS FAITH STRANGE • BARRY SULLIVAN • SULLIVAN • PETE SUMMERS • JENNIE SUMNER • TOM SUTTON • GEMMA SWANN • ALISON SWEET • CAROLINE SWEET • DOUGLAS SWEET • DOUGLAS SWEET • JOAN SWEET • JOAN SWEET • EMMA SWINTON • EMMA SWINTON • SARAH SWINTON • SARAH SWINTON • KAREN SWORD • MIKE SWORD • MORGAN ARWEL SWORD • RHIANYDD MOLLY SWORD • ANTHONY SYMONDS • KEITH SYMONDS • YASMIN SYMONDS • RANGY TANGY • ALYS TAYLOR • BARRY TAYLOR • CERITH ELIS TAYLOR • COLIN TAYLOR • DEAN TAYLOR • DELYTH TAYLOR • DOUGLAS TAYLOR • HELEN TAYLOR • JAN TAYLOR • JESSICA TAYLOR • JOLENE TAYLOR • KATHRYN TAYLOR • LAUREN TAYLOR • M W J TAYLOR • MARTYN TAYLOR • MORGAN THOMAS TAYLOR • RACHEL TAYLOR • RHYS EVAN TAYLOR • SAM TAYLOR • W I TAYLOR • ABBY L TAYLOR • T D W TAYLOR • CHRISTOPHER THAIN • THE GADSBY FAMILY • GEORGE THELWELL • LEWIS THELWELL • SARA THELWELL • SIMON THELWELL • CAROLE THEOBALD • TERRY THEOBALD • ALAN THOMAS • ALUN THOMAS • ALUN THOMAS • ALUN THOMAS • BETHAN THOMAS • BRYTHON OWEN THOMAS • CAROLINE THOMAS • CERI THOMAS • CERI THOMAS • CERIANN THOMAS • CERYS THOMAS • DAVID GERAINT THOMAS • DELYTH NON THOMAS • DERI THOMAS • DES THOMAS • EDWYN THOMAS • EDWYN THOMAS • EILIDH THOMAS • ELIZABETH THOMAS • GARETH THOMAS • GARETH THOMAS • GARETH DAVID THOMAS • GEOFF THOMAS • GEOFF THOMAS • GERWYN THOMAS • GRAHAM THOMAS • GWYNNE THOMAS • HARRI ELLIS THOMAS • HEATHER THOMAS • HEATHER THOMAS • HELENA LOUISA THOMAS • HUGH THOMAS • HUW POWYS THOMAS • JAC ELLIS THOMAS • JADEY THOMAS • JOANNE THOMAS • JOANNE THOMAS • JOHN THOMAS • JOHN ANTHONY THOMAS • JOHN MERRIG THOMAS • KEITH THOMAS • LISA MARIE THOMAS • MANSEL THOMAS • MARK THOMAS • MARK J THOMAS • MARK J THOMAS • MARK S THOMAS • MERFYN THOMAS • MERFYN THOMAS • MIA THOMAS • MYRA THOMAS • OLIVER EDWARD THOMAS • PAULINE THOMAS • POWYS THOMAS • RHIAN THOMAS • RHIAN THOMAS • RHIAN LYNFA THOMAS • ROB THOMAS • ROBERT NEIL THOMAS • ROGER THOMAS • SARAH THOMAS • SHARON LOUISE THOMAS • SLORA THOMAS • TERENCE KEITH THOMAS • VIOLET ROSE THOMAS • THOMAS • YVONNE THOMAS-JONES • ABIGAIL THOMPSON • PETE THOMPSON • WILLIAM THOMPSON • BILL THOMSON • ELSPETH THOMSON • MOIRA THOMSON • SUSAN THOMSON • ALUN THORNE • HARRY THORNE • JAMES THORNE • JENNY THORNE • MATTHEW THORNE • PETER THORNE • STEVE THORNE • SUE THORNE • PAT THORNTON • DAMIAN THURSTON • LEE THURSTON • NIKKI THURSTON • SHANNON THURSTON • KEITH TIBBS • ANN TILAKAWARDANE • KUMARI TILAKAWARDANE • LOUIS TILAKAWARDANE • J-J TILING • LAUREN TIMMONS • LOUISE TIMMONS • [...]AN TIMMONS • ADAM TOD • DANIELLA TOD • JACOB TOD • JOSHUA TOD • SAM TOTTMAN • SIMON TOWNLEY • JEFF TOWNSEND • KEN [...] • RHYS TOWNSEND • RICHARD TOWNSEND • JOSHUA LUKE TRANTER • MARK TRAVERS • JAMIE TUCKER • MANNY TUCKER • MAX [...]MA SHAN TUCKER • OLIVIA DAISY TUCKER • DANIEL TURBERVILLE • SIMON TURBERVILLE • MICHAEL EDWARD TURNER •

THE FANS T-Z

LIAM TUSTIN • ROBERT TYRELL • JOHN TYRRELL • LIA TYRRELL • DAISY VAN OUBRUGGEN • CARWYN VAUGHAN • DAFYDD VAUGHAN • LON VAUGHAN • MIKE VAUGHAN • RHODRI VAUGHAN • ROGER VAUGHAN • STEPHEN VAUGHAN • DAVE VEAL • SYLVAINE VERGEZ • BEN THOMAS WADE • JOHN BRENDAN WADE • WENDY WADE • BETHAN LOWRI WAINFUR • LEE WAINFUR • IEUAN JOHN WAKEFIELD • CHRISTOPHER WAKEFORD • JULIAN WAKEFORD • DANIEL WALBEOFF • DAVE WALBEOFF • RACHEL WALBEOFF • SUE WALBEOFF • DAN WALKER • DAVID MOUSE WALKER • JACQUI WALKER • KEITH WALKER • LOWRI WALKER • OWAIN WALKER • TOMOS WALKER • HEATHER LEIGH WALKER-WYMORE • HUW WALLACE • OWEN WALLACE • SIAN WALLACE • BARRIE WALPOLE • LUCY WALPOLE • HARRY JAMES WALTON • STUART HENRY WALTON • STUART MARK WALTON • LIZ WARD • BRUCE WARNES • DAVE WARRENDER • DAVE WARRENDER • GRANDAD WARRENDER • GRANDAD WARRENDER • LIAM WARRENDER • LIAM WARRENDER • TRISTAN OTTERBIEN & TIMMY WARRENDER • TRISTAN OTTERBIEN &TIMMY WARRENDER • ADRIAN WATERS • RUTH WATERSTON • CALEB WATKINS • CLARE WATKINS • DAFYDD WATKINS • DEAN WATKINS • FAITH WATKINS • EVAN WATTS • IOAN WATTS • MATT WATTS • ROGER WATTS • WAYNE • LIONEL WEAVER • PAT WEAVER • ALEXI WEBB • ANDREAS WEBB • ANDROULLA WEBB • MARTYN WEBB • DAVID WEEKS • EILEEN WEEKS • DEBBIE WEETCH • DYLAN GEORGE WELCH • JAMES WELLER • KIERAN WELLER • OWEN WELLER • BOB WENMAN • KATIE WERNEY • DEE WEST • ANTON WESTACOTT • BRIAN WESTACOTT • LAWRENCE WESTACOTT • MARTIN WESTACOTT • ALASTAIR WHEELHOUSE • ANDREW WHEELHOUSE • BERT WHITBY • JEAN WHITBY • MARK WHITBY • CRAIG WHITCOMBE • EVAN WHITCOMBE • IAN WHITCOMBE • ANGE WHITE • ANGELA WHITE • AURA WHITE • ELLIE ANA WHITE • GARY WHITE • IWAN WHITE • JAMES RHYS WHITE • MARTYN WHITE • RHYS WHITE • THOMAS RHYS WHITE • PAUL JEFFREY WHITE (WAL) • VALMAI WHITEFORD • CHRIS WHITEHEAD • CHRISTOPHER WHITEHEAD • EMMA WHITEHEAD • EMMA WHITEHEAD • FIONA WHITEHEAD • FIONA WHITEHEAD • JONATHAN WHITEHEAD • JONATHAN WHITEHEAD • RICHARD WHITFIELD • TOM WHITMARSH-KNIGHT • IAN WICKS • EDWARD WIGLEY • ELLIOTT WIGLEY • HARRIET WIGLEY • MARTYN WIGLEY • JONATHAN WILCOX • LUCINDA WILCOX • NEIL WILCOX • ANGELA WILDE • DAVID JAMES WILDE • DAVID JAMES WILDE • EMMA WILKINS • DAN WILKS • LISA WILKS • ROB WILKS • SAM WILKS • ALEXANDER WILD DOG WILLEY • ALAN WILLIAMS • ALUN WILLIAMS • AMY WILLIAMS • ANDY WILLIAMS • ANN WILLIAMS • ANN WILLIAMS • BARRIE WILLIAMS • BARRINGTON WILLIAMS • BENJAMIN WILLIAMS • BETHAN WILLIAMS • BETHANY WILLIAMS • BETTINA WILLIAMS • CARWEN HEDD WILLIAMS • CLIVE WILLIAMS • COLIN WILLIAMS • CONOR J R WILLIAMS • D H E WILLIAMS • D H E WILLIAMS • DANIELLE WILLIAMS • DIANE WILLIAMS • ELAINE WILLIAMS • EWAN WILLIAMS • GARETH WILLIAMS • GARETH WILLIAMS • GARETH (GATCHIE) WILLIAMS • GARETH R M WILLIAMS • GAVIN WILLIAMS • GEMMA WILLIAMS • GERWYN LLOYD WILLIAMS • GETHIN RHYS WILLIAMS • GWYN WILLIAMS • GWYN WILLIAMS • HARRY PAUL WILLIAMS • HOWARD C WILLIAMS • HOWARD C WILLIAMS • HYWEL OWEN WILLIAMS • IESTYN WILLIAMS • IOAN WILLIAMS • JACKIE WILLIAMS • JAMIE A SAM WILLIAMS • JANE WILLIAMS • JENNIFE TRACY WILLIAMS • JEREMY WILLIAMS • JEREMY G WILLIAMS • JEREMY G WILLIAMS • JESSICA WILLIAMS • JONATHAN WILLIAMS • JOSHUA WILLIAMS • JULIE WILLIAMS • KAREN WILLIAMS • LES WILLIAMS • LEWIS ANDREW WILLIAMS • LOWRI WILLIAMS • LYNNE WILLIAMS • MARTIN WILLIAMS • MARTIN WILLIAMS • MAUREEN WILLIAMS • MAX WILLIAMS • MEGAN C WILLIAMS • MEGAN C WILLIAMS • MICHELLE WILLIAMS • MORGAN WILLIAMS • NOEL HUW WILLIAMS • O K WILLIAMS • O K WILLIAMS • PAMELA WILLIAMS • PAUL WILLIAMS • PERIS WILLIAMS • PETER WILLIAMS • PHIL WILLIAMS • RHYDIAN WILLIAMS • RHYS WILLIAMS • RHYS WILLIAMS • ROB WILLIAMS • ROBIN WILLIAMS • ROGER WILLIAMS • RYAN WILLIAMS • RYAN LEWIS WILLIAMS • SANDRA WILLIAMS • SARAH WILLIAMS • SARAN HAF WILLIAMS • SAUL WILLIAMS • SEREN WILLIAMS • SEREN WILLIAMS • SHANE WILLIAMS • SOPHIE WILLIAMS • STEPH WILLIAMS • STEPH WILLIAMS • SYLVIA M WILLIAMS • SYLVIA M WILLIAMS • TAFF WILLIAMS • TELERI FFLYR WILLIAMS • WILLIAMS • DAVID JOHN WILLIAMS • IFOR WILLIS • BRIAN WILSON • COLIN WILSON • DONALD WILSON • ELLIOT WINTER • LINDA WINTER • MICHAEL WINTER • ANDREW WOOD • BAILEY WOOD • EMILY WOOD • NIGEL WOOD • SAM WOOD • SARAH WOOD • ANTHONY WOODS • CAROL WOODS • PETE WOODS • OWEN THOMAS WOOLDRIDGE • AMELIA WORSLEY • ANGHARAD WORSLEY • LAWRENCE WORSLEY • SIAN WORSLEY • CLAIRE WYATT • EMILY WYATT • LOTTIE WYATT • SIMON WYATT • GLENN WM WYMORE • WILLIAM D W WYMORE • SEREN WYN • WILLIAM WYN BIFFIN • MANON WYN DAVIES • MYRFYN WYN DAVIES • ANGHARAD WYN EVANS • ALYS WYN GRIFFITHS • FFION WYN GRIFFITHS • GARETH WYN GRIFFITHS • DEWI WYN HUGHES • HOWARD WYN HUGHES • DEWI WYN JONES • ELA + ARWEL WYNN WILLIAMS • CAI YEOMAN • HARRISON YEOMAN • JAMIE YEOMAN • JAMIE LLOYD YEOMAN • MABLI HEDD YEOMAN • OWEN LLYWD YEOMAN • RACHAEL YEOMAN • JUN YOSHIDA • SHIN YOSHIDA • DAVE YOUNG • DAVID YOUNG • GARETH YOUNG • JENNY YOUNG • OWEN YOUNG

THANK YOU FOR YOUR SUPPORT
DIOLCH AM EICH CEFNOGAETH

GERAINT ALEXANDER • JOHN ALI • PAUL ALI • CHRIS ALLEN • DAVID ARTHUR • SOPHIE BENNETT • GWYN BRACE
LIZA BURGESS • PAUL BUTTERWORTH • FIONA BYRNE • CRAIG CAMPBELL • MARC CARTER • JAMES CHAPRON
DIANE CLARK • CHRIS CORNFORD • BEN CORNISH • ANDREW COX • DARREN CROSSMAN • IOAN CUNNINGHAM
BEN DANIELS • DAVID DAVIES • EMMA DAVIES • GARETH A DAVIES • GARETH DAVIES • GEOFF DAVIES • LLYR DAVIES
MARC DAVIES • RHYS EDWARDS • ADRIAN EVANS • JONATHAN EVANS • LEE EVANS • TERRY EVANS • JULIAN FERRARI
PAUL FISHER • RICHARD FRENCH • KATIE GARDINER • JON GARDNER • KEVIN GEORGE • MIKE GIBBONS
GRAEME GILLESPIE • LAURA GOODE • DUANE GOODFIELD • ANGELA GREAVES • NADINE GRIFFITHS • JADE HANLEY
MARCIA HARDING • ROB HARES • RYAN HARRIS • LYNN HARWOOD • ANN HAWKINS • BYRON HAYWARD
DAVID HIGGS • JANET HILL • CHRISTIAN HITT • TIM HOARE • GARRY HOBBS • RICHARD HODGES • KEITH HOLLIFIELD
CHRIS HORSMAN • NATALIE HUGHES • HELEN IHENACHO • ROBERT IMPEY • ANDREW JAMES • ASHLEY JAMES
CAROLINE JAMES • GEMMA JAMES • CLAIRE JENKINS • DAI JENKINS • DUNCAN JOHN • PAUL JOHN • PHIL JOHN
ANDREW JONES • CARWYN JONES • CLIVE JONES • GARETH JONES • GETHIN JONES • JAMES JONES • LISA JONES
LIZ JONES • LYN JONES • MALCOLM JONES • REBECCA JONES • MARC KINNAIRD • NEIL LATIMER • ALAN LEWIS
ALLAN LEWIS • CAROLINE LEWIS • CARWYN LEWIS • GARETH LEWIS • GERAINT LEWIS • JASON LEWIS • RHODRI LEWIS
ROGER LEWIS • JULIE LINDSAY • JONNY LLEWHELLIN • TRACEY LLOYD • JUSTIN LLOYD • ALEX LUFF • JOE LYDON
CRAIG MALONEY • CHRIS MAPSTONE • CARLY MATTHEWS • CRAIG MAXWELL • CLAIRE MCADAM • TERENCE MCGARRY
DAMIAN MCGRATH • KEVIN MCGUCKIAN • DALE MCINTOSH • PHIL MEADON • CARA MIFFLIN • ANTONY MILES
ANDREW MILLWARD • STEWART MILNE • NATALIE MOCK • CAROLINE MORGAN • CERYS MORGAN • TIM MOSS
KATE MYNOTT • SARAH NASH • DEBORAH NICHOLAS • PETER OWEN • CHRISSIE OWENS • DANIEL OWENS
NIGEL OWENS • PETER OWENS • CHRIS PAGLIONICO • ANTHONY PALMER • JULIE PATERSON • MARTYN PAYNE
IAN PEPLOE • STEVE PHILLIPS • CRAIG PHILLIPS • DAVID PICKERING • STACEY PITMAN • JOANNA PLUMMER
LYNNE PRICE • WAYNE PROCTOR • LENA RANN • JOHN REES • JOSH REES • MARTYN REES • DARYL RICHARDS
JEFF ROACH • EIFION ROBERTS • GERRY ROBERTS • MARC ROBERTS • EMMA ROGERS • MARK ROLLINGS • BEN ROSE
NICK ROSE • SIMON ROWE • MITCHELL SALES • JIM SALISBURY • ROSS SALMON • SARAH SAMUEL • NIGEL SAUNDERS
CARL SCALES • BRIAN SCOTT • LIAM SCOTT • LYNNE SCOTT • MATT SILVA • THOMAS SLOANE • NICOLA SMITH
STEVE SMITH • RAOUL STEVENSON • TOM SUTTON • HOWARD SWAN • MARK TAYLOR • ADRIAN THOMAS
ALAN THOMAS • ANDREW THOMAS • AUSTIN THOMAS • EILIDH THOMAS • JULIE THOMAS • LEAH THOMAS
MICHAEL THOMAS • TONY THOMAS • WILL THOMAS • STACEY THOMPSON • GERALD TOMS • RYAN TOMS • ROSS TRISTRAM
LEIGH TURNER • JILL WALTERS • GETHIN WATTS • NIGEL WAY • NIGEL WHITEHOUSE • TOM WHITMARSH-KNIGHT
SIMON WHITTAM • SOPHIE WILKINSON • DANIELLE WILKS • PAUL WILLETTS • AMANDA WILLIAMS • ANDY WILLIAMS
CHRIS WILLIAMS • GARETH WILLIAMS • JOHN WILLIAMS • MICHAEL WILLIAMS • RHODRI WILLIAMS • VICTORIA WILLIAMS
• CHRISTINA WILLIAMSON • DANNY WILSON • ANTHONY WRIDE • STEPHEN WRIDE • ROBERT YEMAN

GRANDSLAMS

1909 1911 1950 1952 1971 1976 1978 2005 2008 2012

WRU

GRANDSLAM
CHAMPIONS 2012

GRAND SLAM
CHAMPIONS

1908
1911
1909
1950 1952
1971
1978 1976
2008 2005
2012